BIG
TAX
SAVINGS
For Small Business

Joseph R. Oliver

ISBN: 0-913864-68-4

Library of Congress Catalog Card No. 82-71426

First Printing, July 1982
Second Printing (Revised), January 1983
Third Printing, July 1983

Published by: Enterprise Publishing, Inc.
725 Market Street
Wilmington, Delaware 19801

I am indebted to Patti Cleary for her fine editorial comments and suggestions and to Ed Roach for his continuing encouragement.

To James, Elsie, and Letty Oliver

Table of Contents

PART FIVE: Low-Tax Disposals of Assets

Preface

Tax Advantages of Owning Your Own Business

If you own a business, you are in one of the best of all possible situations for saving taxes. If you are thinking about starting or buying a business, the valuable tax advantages ownership affords will serve to encourage you to get started.

Throughout the history of this country, Congress has favored the small business. Although most people are not aware of it, tax law (written by Congress) gives special consideration to the small enterprise.

As a result, businesses have access to a great number of excellent tax breaks. And almost all of them are available to the average small business owner. You don't need to be rich to save taxes.

Exactly how effective can you expect these tax breaks to be?

- Any of them can cut your income taxes.
- Several may be able to virtually eliminate your taxes.
- And using as many of them as you can in combination will devastate your tax bill—squeezing the maximum benefit out of the tax-saving opportunities available to you.

When tax breaks reduce or even completely wipe out your obligation to the Internal Revenue Service (IRS), it is all perfectly legal. As the famous Judge Learned Hand said:

> . . . there is nothing sinister in so arranging one's affairs as to keep taxes as low as possible. Everybody does so, rich or poor;

and all do right, for nobody owes any public duty to pay more than the law demands: taxes are enforced extractions, not voluntary contributions.

Tax-Saving Opportunities Are Better

If tax breaks this good are available to average folks, why don't more people use them?

First of all, many forward-looking people *do* employ these tax-savings techniques to save large amounts of taxes.

Secondly, individuals who fail to use them are often eligible for numerous tax breaks, but simply do not take the time to learn what can be done to save taxes.

Lastly, the tax breaks available to business owners are far greater in number and generosity than those which can be used by people who work as employees of others. Businesses are faced with a wide selection of ways in which to save taxes. A business owner must know which of these tax-cutting methods will benefit him the most.

In fact, the tax-saving opportunities available to businesses are so good and so numerous that if you do not currently own a business, these special deals can help you make up your mind. Who can resist the prospect of a company car, home office deductions, fringe benefits, tax-sheltered retirement plans, capital gains, accelerated depreciation, and other benefits tax law gives to businesses?

If you already have a business—whether it is a sole proprietorship, partnership, or corporation—you can probably save more taxes now than you ever have in the past.

Businesses Have More Deductions

From travel and entertainment and retirement plans to rapid depreciation, business owners are able to take more deductions than can people who do not work for themselves. If you're self-employed, numerous items (which you could not otherwise use on your tax return) suddenly become deductible. And other expenses move to positions on your return where they can provide greater tax savings.

Deductions are the bread and butter of a good tax-reduction program.

Several chapters of this book explain how to best use specific tax deductions. And Chapter 5 lists most of the different business deductions to which you are entitled, giving important facts about each.

Details Worth Your Attention

In addition to finding extra deductions with a business, you can better save taxes by using certain tax tricks. These are perfectly legal ways to cut your taxes by doing practically nothing. Most people aren't aware of them.

For example, just the way you or your accountant record revenues and expenses may allow you to postpone taxes on your income. Splitting your business earnings with your family can reduce your overall tax bill. And something as simple as the way you think of your inventory may have a dramatic impact on the taxes you pay.

These are facts most people would ignore. Yet they can save you an enormous amount of taxes with hardly any effort. Chapters 6, 7, and 8 explain them in detail.

How Taxes Affect Businesses Differently

The form of business organization you choose (sole proprietorship, partnership, Subchapter S corporation, or regular corporation) can also affect your tax bill.

Sole proprietorships and partnerships are flexible and easy to start. But they have legal disadvantages and can sometimes result in your paying more taxes than you would if your business were organized as a corporation.

The Subchapter S corporation is extremely useful under specific circumstances, but can be a hindrance in other cases.

You would be surprised to see how easily an ordinary corporation can reduce taxes in many business situations. The tax rates applied to your profits may actually be lower. You can sell assets to your corporation tax-free. And the list of deductible fringe benefits seems endless.

If you aren't currently president of your own corporation, you may be passing up numerous tax-saving opportunities. If you already own a corporation, you are probably not taking advantage of anywhere near the total number of tax breaks which are available to you.

Chapters 9, 10, 11, and 12 give you the straight facts about different forms of business organization and how to save taxes with each.

Cutting Your Taxes With Business Assets

While you should be careful not to purchase more than your business needs, the simple act of buying assets can reduce your income tax bill. If you want, generous depreciation deductions and tax credits can even help you to completely eliminate your taxes year after year.

Your own business building, or perhaps just a few rental houses, can provide you with tax shelter you have only dreamed about. Special improvements to and rehabilitations of buildings can further enhance the coverage of your income.

And careful timing of your purchase of cars, airplanes, furniture, and other assets may save you more than enough taxes to make the down payments on them.

Tax law again helps you when you wish to dispose of business assets. Special types of trades and sales may keep you from paying any taxes on gains or permit you to postpone your tax bills on them. If you do owe taxes, using a little-known technique for mixing capital gains and losses can minimize your debt to the IRS.

Chapters 13 through 21 show you how to use business property to save more taxes than you have ever thought possible.

How to Best the IRS

Eventually, the whole tax-saving process comes down to beating the IRS at its own game—or at least staying one step ahead of them.

Tax traps, tax investigations, and tax audits are aimed at innocent as well as guilty people. It is wise for anyone to make a point of knowing the facts about these possible annoyances.

You'll want to know where the tax traps are hidden and what you can do to avoid them, how the IRS can spot unreported income, and what is the best way to handle a tax audit. Chapters 22, 23, and 24 give you the information you need. Then Chapter 25 shows you how to choose and use a tax advisor, including how to get the best services for less money.

Important Points

How many staightforward, plain-language books about specific ways to save taxes in your business have you seen lately?

They *are* rare, aren't they?

That is exactly why this book was written.

Businesses have access to numerous tax breaks which are not being discussed with business owners. This book explains most of the business tax advantages currently available and shows how each can be used in *your* business.

You will see:

1) The awesome variety of business deductions you can take on your tax return.

2) Those special tax tricks which only a business can use to save taxes with virtually no effort.

3) Why choosing the proper form of business organization can save more taxes than you think.

4) How knowing which assets to own, when to buy them, and the best ways to dispose of them can completely change your tax return.

5) The best ways to avoid hassles with the IRS but beat them if you meet them.

As long as you are already self-employed or plan to start or buy your own business, you might as well use to the fullest the special tax status you have. At the least, you will be able to save income taxes every year. At the most, you can completely eliminate your taxes with perfectly legal business tax breaks.

And, importantly, every business decision you make during the year can be made with an eye for the tax consequences. The IRS patiently waits at your door. This book is designed to help you avoid making the mistakes for which they watch.

PART ONE

Your Wide Selection of Deductions

1

Higher Auto, Travel, and Entertainment Deductions

Few businesses can operate without a certain amount of expenditures each year for autos, travel, and entertainment. Automobile expense is needed in order to move employees and products around your city or area. Travel costs (including public transportation, meals, and lodging) are necessary for out-of-town business trips.

Entertainment, such as the purchase of meals and beverages for clients or customers, employees, and business associates, seems to 1) help deals come together more easily, 2) build your business more quickly, and 3) promote goodwill among those who can help your enterprise run smoothly.

Congress recognizes that these are necessary costs of doing business and allows generous deductions for them. Since some people have taken unwarranted liberties with these deductions, guidelines must now be followed if you want to use them on your tax return. But, these costs are still a valuable source of deductions for anyone who is willing to play the game by the rules.

Tax Breaks for Autos and Transportation

For your business auto, you can deduct either 1) depreciation on each vehicle plus the actual out-of-pocket operating costs or 2) an arbitrary amount per mile you drive it. Only one of the two methods can be used to figure your annual deduction. When you begin to use a car in your business, you can quickly estimate what your deductions will be for the next couple of years with each method. Then use the one which gives the higher deduction.

Depreciation and Out-of-Pocket Costs

Unless you plan to drive a considerable number of miles each year, depreciation and actual costs of operating a vehicle will yield a larger deduction in the first few years than will the mileage method. If your business owns two or more automobiles, you'll probably be required by the Internal Revenue Service (IRS) to use this method.

The first thing you do is calculate depreciation with Table A shown on the following page. Note that tax law says you will depreciate your car or light-duty truck over three years.

For example, your purchase of a $10,000 car in 1983 or later would result in 25 percent of its cost ($2,500) becoming depreciation in the year you buy it. You get the entire $2,500 deduction whether you acquire the vehicle in January or December. Your second year's depreciation would be 38% of cost ($3,800). Your deduction in the third year would be 37% ($3,700).

If you are *really* in need of some tax-saving deductions, you might consider expensing a large part of the cost of your auto (Chapter 15). For example, your depreciation for the year you bought the car above turned out to be $2,500. By using the new expensing option, you might raise your first year's depreciation to $6,250.

And don't forget to take investment credit on it (Chapter 16). The credit on a $10,000 vehicle would be $600. That is $600 knocked directly off your tax bill—almost enough for your down payment on the auto.

After calculating depreciation, the next step is to total your out-of-.pocket costs. You add gasoline, oil, repairs, insurance, licenses,

Table A Depreciating Cars and Light-Duty Trucks

Percentage You Apply to Vehicle's Cost	
Year of Use	Auto Put Into Use January 1, 1981 or Later
1	25%
2	38%
3	37%
	100%

interests, tolls, parking, and any other costs of operating your car or truck. Then, the total of depreciation plus out-of-pocket costs becomes your deduction for the year.

Let's say that you buy a $12,000 car in 1984. Your first year's depreciation would be 25 percent of the cost, or $3,000. We might guess your total deduction to stack up as follows:

Cost	Amount
Depreciation	$3,000
Gasoline	900
Oil	50
Repairs	150
Insurance	400
Taxes	200
Interest	1,200
Tolls & Parking	75
Licenses	50
Total Deduction (for 1984)	$6,025

Taking investment credit reduces slightly your depreciation deduction. In the case of a vehicle, only 97 percent of its cost can be depreciated across the three years. Your $3,000 depreciation deduction above would be reduced to $2,910 (97 percent of $3,000).

Mileage Method

The mileage method allows you to deduct a specific amount for each mile you drive your vehicle during the year. In addition to this total, you can also deduct interest, tolls, parking, and taxes other than gasoline taxes. But you can't deduct depreciation or any of the other expenses listed above. The mileage allowance takes their place.

Normally, you could benefit from the mileage method only if you drive a considerable number of miles each year. Currently, this method might give you larger deductions if you drive a vehicle more than 30,000 to 40,000 miles each year. But if you buy a car to drive only 5,000 to 10,000 miles per year, the depreciation and actual costs method will give you better tax breaks in the first few years of ownership.

Since the cost of operating a vehicle keeps going up, the IRS occasionally increases the amount of expense they allow for each mile you drive. You can find out the rate to use for any specific year by calling your nearest IRS office (see Appendix F at the end of this book for toll-free IRS telephone numbers) or your tax advisor.

Since you may be asked to prove your total mileage for a year, be sure to keep a "log" of dates the car is used, locations visited, reasons for visits, and mileage. See Appendix A at the end of this book for a sample mileage log.

Part Business, Part Pleasure

If your automobile is used for both business and personal purposes, you'll be able to deduct only the costs of operating it for your business. Most of the nonbusiness part is not deductible.

When you use the mileage method, this doesn't present a problem. You only record in the log your business miles.

But, if you use the depreciation plus actual out-of-pocket costs method, you'll need to allocate your costs between business and personal use. In the example we used for the depreciation and actual costs method, we assumed that your total vehicle costs for a year were $6,025. Using the auto 60 percent for business and 40 percent for pleasure would mean that 60 percent of the total, or $3,615, would be deductible as a business expense. Of the other 40 percent, your taxes and interest could be deducted as itemized deductions. The remainder would not be deductible at all.

When you use a vehicle only partly for business, and figure your deduction with the depreciation plus actual costs method, you might want to keep a log of trips and mileage. In the event of a tax audit, it could help prove your business percentage (60%, 50%, 80%, or whatever) for the year.

Public Transportation

When you use your automobile on an out-of-town business trip, your deduction is figured the same as always. You take either depreciation plus actual costs or the mileage allowance. If you're already using the depreciation method, your trip will just add gasoline and other costs to your total for the year. If you are following the mileage method, your miles for the year are increased.

When you take a plane, train, or other public transportation, the actual cost of your ticket, cab fares, and other similar costs are deductible. Be sure to record the amounts of your expenditures, dates, places, people talked to, and business purpose of each trip. This may require more time, but the extra taxes you'll save with good records will be worth the effort. You will probably not forget to deduct that $16.25 cab trip in Cleveland nor will you be as likely to lose the deduction for it in the event of an audit. (A sample expense diary is provided as Appendix B at the end of this book.)

Making the Most of Meals and Lodging

The actual costs of meals and lodging are deductible for out-of-town business trips if you are away from home long enough to get a room and rest. This doesn't necessarily have to be two days away from home, but it should be longer than a normal work day.

For example, let us say that you fly to another city at 8 a.m. and return at 6 p.m. the same day. Although you're out of town all day, you probably are not gone long enough to get a room and rest. So, none of your meals is deductible. The IRS sees your meals as having the same status as those you eat in your home town—nondeductible personal living expenses.

On the other hand, if you leave on a plane at 3 a.m. and return at midnight, you might take a room for a few hours' rest. If you do, all your meals and lodging are probably deductible.

This may seem to be an odd way to distinguish between meals that are deductible and those that aren't. But the IRS wants you to be out of town long enough to get a room and rest before you call your meals a business expense.

So, if you are planning to spend two separate days in another city, try to schedule them so that one immediately follows the other. Rather than leaving and returning the same day on two different occasions, conduct business one day, stay overnight, then conduct more business the next day. You will meet the IRS test and your meals and lodging will be deductible.

How to Deduct Entertainment

Of course, meals in your home city or out of town can be deducted anytime if they qualify as entertainment expense.

Here, again, people have abused deductions until tax rules got tighter. But the alert person can still save taxes with his entertainment costs.

The first thing you'll want to be sure of is that you spend your entertainment dollar with the idea that your business will benefit from the expenditure. You may never be audited by the IRS (Chapter 24). But, if you are, you will want your entertainment deductions to be on solid footing.

How do you do this?

Try to talk business before, during, or after every entertainment occasion for which you pay. If you buy a "quiet business meal" for someone, you do not have to discuss business. But stay away from noisy bars. The IRS wants the surroundings during the meal to be conducive to talking business.

Carefully record whom you entertain, their titles and company affiliations, the place and time of entertainment, the amount you spent, and what you discussed. (This really is not the burden it seems. In fact, a few credit card receipts have forms on the back for recording this information. If yours don't, keep a diary of entertainment expenses.)

Always pay by check or credit card when possible. Trying to remember cash outlays later is very difficult.

Business Gifts

In addition to entertainment, you may sometimes find that gifts to customers or prospective customers help build your business. Especially during holiday seasons, you will find that gifts of bottles of beverages, turkeys, hams, fruit baskets, and jewelry are common.

But be careful how much you give to any one person. You can deduct up to only $25 of gifts per person per year. For example, whether you give a customer a $25 turkey or a $500 TV, your deduction for the gift is limited to $25.

Fortunately, you do not need to consider the costs of shipping, gift wrapping, engraving of jewelry, and other incidental costs. Just the cost of each gift itself must be $25 or less.

Although the annual limit of gifts to each customer is $25, you can give more expensive gifts to employees if the gift is for the employee's productivity, length of service, or safety achievement. The gift must be "tangible personal property," such as jewelry, sporting equipment, luggage, or similar items.

The annual limit of gifts to each employee (deductible by you, but *not* taxed to the employee) is $400. If you have a permanent written plan or program for them, the value of gifts can go as high as $1,600 per employee each year as long as the average gift costs no more than $400. Be sure not to tilt the program in favor of owners or highly-paid employees.

Many devices have been tried as motivational tools—money, increased participation in management, more comfortable working conditions, flexible working hours, and others. But a simple tax-free gift costing up to $400 (or $1,600) for productivity, length of service, or safety has to rank near the top.

For every gift you make, you will need to briefly jot down whom you gave it to, his title, your business relationship, the reason for the gift, the date, and the cost of the gift. You might never be audited. But, if you are, you'll want to keep all your tax-saving deductions. Records will help you to do this. (See Appendix C at the end of this book.)

Your Records Are Critical

Since entertainment, travel, and related deductions have been so abused by people in the past, the IRS is jumpy about them. Receipts are now required except for the smallest expenditures. Your expense diary will provide the documentation you need for the small ones.

The reason this chapter has stressed records is that during a tax audit, the burden of proof will be on you. You'll be proving that your deductions *were* proper. The IRS won't have to prove that they *were not*. The better your records are, the easier your job will be.

Deductions do not save taxes. *Provable* deductions save taxes. Try to acquire the habit of making each expenditure a solid deduction.

"It's Deductible" (Or Is It?)

People often get in the habit of spending lavishly for business entertainment, meals, lodging, and travel with the idea that "It's deductible." The problem with this reasoning is that someone in the 40 percent tax bracket may cut 40 cents off his taxes with every $1 of deduction. But the other 60 cents comes out of his own pocket. If he goes up against a hard-bitten IRS agent, the whole $1 may come out of his own pocket.

It often takes cash to get the tax-saving deductions and credits explained in other chapters of this book. Each dollar you keep in your pocket by avoiding lavish entertainment and other expenses may be able to save you even more taxes somewhere else.

For example, you can use cash as a down payment on a computer or business auto, then take investment credit (Chapter 16) and rapid depreciation (Chapter 15) on the asset's entire cost. Putting $1,000 into entertainment might get you a $1,000 tax deduction. But using the same $1,000 as a down payment on a business auto might get you as much as $5,000 or $10,000 of deductions for the year.

The next time you are tempted to say "It's deductible," stop a moment to think about the tax-saving alternatives.

Important Points

Most businesses have at least some expenditures for auto expenses, travel, meals, lodging, and entertainment each year. These are part of the daily costs required to run a business smoothly and to build revenues. As long as you've got to spend the money, you might as well use these costs to save as much taxes as possible. You can do this by following a few basic rules:

1) When there are two ways to figure a deduction (such as auto expenses), be sure you are using the more profitable method;

2) Do not spend money unless you're pretty sure you will get a deduction for it;

3) Try to structure your trips so that you can deduct your meals and lodging;

4) When in doubt, talk business;

5) Watch the size of those business gifts carefully;

6) Keep receipts and records.

Uncle Sam wants to help you save taxes with your business expenses. If you'd like him to help you as much as possible, be sure to keep his rules in mind.

2

Deducting Your Home Office

One way to hold down overhead when you start a business, especially a part-time business, is to conduct its operations in your home. Several companies with annual sales currently above $100 million started 10 or 15 years ago in garages or basements.

Some people find it convenient to operate a business out of their home indefinitely. As commuting, rent, and other costs rise, experts predict an increase in the number of home-based enterprises.

Even if you have a commercial location for your business, you may find yourself making phone calls, preparing advertising copy, reviewing contracts, having discussions with clients, and completing other tasks at home.

However you use your home for business purposes, you should consider the tax-saving potential of the home office deduction.

Which Costs Are Deductible?

If you structure the use of your residence so that you qualify for the home office deduction, you'll want to be sure to carefully collect receipts on all expenses allowed. Cancelled checks can be very useful in proving expenditures.

Naturally, your interest, taxes, and casualty losses are deductible. In addition to these, you may be able to deduct part of your insurance, repairs, utilities, maid's wages, and other costs of the residence. If customers or clients visit your home frequently for business reasons, you may even be able to deduct part of your lawn-care expenditures.

By owning your own home, you can add depreciation to these other expenses. If you rent, part of the rent you pay will take the place of depreciation.

The costs of a business telephone would normally be completely deductible. Using your residence phone partly for business would require a division of its cost between personal (nondeductible) and business (deductible) use.

Type of Office You Need

In order to deduct expenses for business use of your home, you'll need to set aside a specific portion of the residence (such as a room or rooms) for your business. This room or rooms can't be used for anything else. You cannot store clothing in them or play cards there. Your kids won't be able to watch TV in them. They are strictly reserved for business.

The business area of your home must be used on a regular basis either as your principal place of business or as a place for meeting with clients, customers, or patients.

But the business for which you are using your home does not have to be a full-time occupation. You can have more than one trade or business—one of them justifying a deduction for use of your residence.

If you aren't self-employed, any use of your home must be for your employer's convenience, not your own.

The IRS point of view is that if you're serious about your enterprise and the time that you put into it, you will not mind setting aside an area for nothing but business use. Tax law does not require large amounts of office furnishings. But some office furniture and file cabinets, and perhaps a business phone, can increase your efficiency while making both your customers and the IRS more comfortable.

Investment credit (Chapter 16) and rapid depreciation (Chapter 15) can be taken on furnishings and equipment.

Figuring Your Deduction

The idea behind home office deductions is that part of the costs of running your entire residence are due to business activities and part to personal use. So, the total amount of several expenses must be divided between personal and business use.

How should they be divided?

For most costs, you can use the ratio of the square feet used for business to the total square feet of your home.

For example, let's say that you use two rooms with a total of 400 square feet for business in a 2,000 square-foot house. In this case, 20 percent (400 divided by 2,000) of expenses would be business expenses.

The other 80 percent would be for personal use of your dwelling. Of that 80 percent, you could deduct interest, taxes, and casualty losses as itemized deductions. But the remainder of this 80 percent would be nondeductible living expenses.

Costs for a year might be broken down as follows:

	Total Costs	Business 20%	Nonbusiness 80%
Property taxes	$ 2,000	$ 400	$1,600
Interest	3,000	600	2,400
Insurance	500	100	400
Utilities	1,500	300	1,200
Ordinary repairs	700	140	560
Depreciation	1,800	360	1,440
Maid's wages	1,000	200	800
Totals	$10,500	$2,100	$8,400

Of the $10,500 total costs of running your home this year, 20 percent ($2,100) is because of business use. The other 80 percent is from personal use.

How the Limits Work

To determine your total home office deduction for a year, you must first figure the amount of gross income which probably results from business use of your residence. For the sake of our example, let's say that this is $1,500 of revenue for the year.

From this $1,500, you now subtract the business part of interest, taxes, and casualty losses on your home. Since there were not any casualty losses in the breakdown of expenses above, we need only add up 20 percent of your interest and taxes. The total is $1,000 ($400 of taxes plus $600 interest). Subtracting $1,000 from your $1,500 of revenue leaves $500.

From this remaining $500 of revenue, you can subtract your other office expenses. But you can't subtract more than the $500.

In our example, remaining home office costs amount to $1,100 (insurance, $100; utilities, $300; ordinary repairs, $140; depreciation, $360; and maid's wages, $200). Since only $500 of revenue was left after you subtracted interest and taxes, you will only be able to deduct $500 of this $1,100. The rest cannot be deducted at all.

Your total home office deduction for the year is $1,500 ($1,000 of interest and taxes, plus $500 of the remaining costs).

If $2,000 had remained after subtracting interest, taxes, and casualties, you could have subtracted up to $2,000 of other office costs. So, you'd be able to deduct the entire $1,100 in our example. If $-0- had remained, you could not have deducted *any* more. (Notice that this limit applies only to home office expenses. You'll still probably be able to deduct your auto and other costs without limit.)

Revenue generated by use of your home	$1,000	$1,500	$3,000
Interest	(600)	(600)	(600)
Taxes ....ь.........	(400)	(400)	(400)
Remainder (maximum amount of other home office expenses you can deduct)	$ -0-	$ 500	$2,000

Be Sure to Deduct All These Costs

Property taxes, interest, and casualty losses are deductible whether or not any revenue is generated by using your dwelling for business purposes. If your $1,500 of revenue above had been $-0-, you could have used all your interest and taxes as an itemized deduction.

As the example turned out, $1,000 of interest and taxes became part of your total home office deduction. This left $4,000 ($1,600 of property taxes and $2,400 of interest) in the non-business 80 percent column. Do not forget to use this $4,000 as part of your itemized deductions for the year. Even though they are not business deductions, property taxes, interest, and casualty losses qualify as itemized deductions.

Unfortunately, the nonbusiness 80 percent of your other housing costs (insurance, utilities, repairs, depreciation, maid's wages, and others) can't be deducted at all.

Paying Yourself Rent and Deducting It

As you will see in Chapter 9, having your business taxed as a corporation can result in double taxation of business income—once when the corporation files its tax return and again when you pay dividends to yourself. You may be able to save taxes by paying rent to yourself for business use of your home.

How would this work?

As long as your corporation is using part of your residence for business purposes, it should logically pay you rent. Right?

And rent is an expense to the corporation, much as salary or interest is. Your corporation deducts it. Since rent is paid to you, it is taxed to you as income. But you've got your home office deduction to offset this income. So, you are virtually "milking" tax-free dollars out of your corporation.

Chapters 9 and 11 will go into more detail about this and other ways to take cash out of your corporation before its taxes are figured.

Important Points

When you sell your personal residence, you can normally avoid any taxes on the gain by buying or building a more expensive one within two years. One problem that you could eventually face as a result of taking depreciation on a home office is that you might pay taxes on part of such a gain. Weighing this possibility against a reduction of taxes year after year with the home office deduction will probably lead most people to take the deduction now and risk some taxes later.

A little forethought is required to structure the use of your home so that the business portion of your household expenses can go to your tax return. Carefully set aside a room or rooms and use them for nothing but business. If your home isn't your principal place of business, you should use it for meeting with some clients or customers. You can bolster your case for the home office deduction by keeping a record of who visits your home when and for what purpose.

Keep receipts and/or cancelled checks for all expenses of your residence so that you can easily prove the types and amounts of expenditures.

A business phone and selected pieces of office furniture may help demonstrate your intention to seriously use your home for business purposes. But nothing caps your proof like generating revenues. And the revenues you make from using your home may even determine how much you can deduct of expenses other than interest, taxes, and casualties.

People often use their homes for business purposes more than they think. Since the business part of your household costs can amount to a surprising total, the home office deduction is a tax-saving item which you shouldn't overlook.

3

Theft and Casualty Losses

Sooner or later, almost everyone is the victim of some type of theft or casualty. Storms and other disasters occur with unsettling frequency. Burglaries and thefts are increasing at an alarming rate, and the recovery of stolen property seems to have become more and more difficult.

It is possible, when insurance and other proceeds are taken into account, to have a gain from a theft or casualty. Such a gain can usually be postponed by following involuntary conversion rules (Chapter 17).

But, as inflation continues, people often discover after thefts or casualties that their insurance coverage wasn't adequate. In these cases, the result can be a large loss.

Luckily, tax law lets you take the sting out of your loss by deducting it. No one is happy to have a theft or casualty loss, but at least you can turn each one into a tax-saving device.

What a Casualty Is

To be deductible, a loss must be due to an unusual, sudden, or unexpected event such as a theft, fire, flood, tornado, hail, earthquake, volcano, or wreck. Progressive deterioration of property (by definition, not "sudden") cannot cause a deductible loss. So, termite damage, dry rot, or gradual erosion of land are rarely deductible.

For example, let's say that a warehouse you own is damaged by termites. Although a few people have won deductions for similar losses by going to court, the official IRS stance is that yours can't be deducted.

On the other hand, fire, storm, or other damage to your warehouse would qualify as a casualty. And a loss on the theft or wreck of your car would also be deductible.

You Won't Always Have a Loss

The idea of a casualty or theft always conjurs up the image of a loss—never a gain. But you are just as likely to have a gain on a theft or casualty involving business property as you are to have a loss.

Why?

Productive business property is depreciated. The total of this depreciation is subtracted from an asset's cost and the *result* (not the cost) is compared to the insurance or other proceeds you receive.

Assume, for instance, that you buy a business car for $12,000. You quickly take $9,000 of depreciation over just a few years. When depreciation is subtracted from cost, the result is a $3,000 "adjusted basis" ($12,000 cost, less $9,000 of depreciation). If your insurance company pays you $4,000 because the car is stolen, you have a $1,000 *gain* ($4,000 insurance proceeds, less $3,000 adjusted basis). You *don't* have an $8,000 loss ($4,000 insurance proceeds, less $12,000 cost).

	Correct	Incorrect
Insurance Recovery	$ 4,000	$ 4,000
Less: Adjusted Basis ($12,000 − $9,000)	3,000	
Less: Cost		$12,000
Gain (Loss)	$1,000	($ 8,000)

But an insurance settlement of $1,800 would give you a loss. Subtracting your $3,000 adjusted basis from the $1,800 proceeds would give you a deductible loss of $1,200.

Insurance Recovery	$ 1,800
Less: Adjusted Basis ($12,000 − $9,000)	3,000
Loss	($ 1,200)

How to Figure Your Loss

When a business asset is involved in a theft or casualty, the way your loss is figured will depend on whether the item is 1) partially destroyed or 2) completely destroyed. Since you lose the whole asset, we'll assume that a theft is complete destruction.

Partial Destruction

When business property is just injured, rather than completely destroyed, you compare the smaller of two numbers to insurance or other recovery to find your loss. The two numbers are 1) the decline in fair market value resulting from the casualty or 2) the cost or other basis of the item.

In the example above of the automobile, the adjusted basis was $3,000 ($12,000 cost, less $9,000 of depreciation). This figure has nothing to do with the car's actual fair market value, which could be $10,000 or $1,500 or anything else. Depreciation may or may not reflect the day-to-day decline in an asset's value. It is not designed to do so. And it probably won't, especially if you use the maximum depreciation deduction to which you're entitled.

Let us say that the car's fair market value was $3,500 before a hailstorm, but was only $2,100 afterward. The decline in value because of the storm would be $1,400 ($3,500, less $2,100).

If this is the case, the smaller of 1) the decline in fair maket value ($1,400) or 2) the item's adjusted basis ($3,000) is the number compared to your insurance recovery. Of the two, the decline in fair market value is smaller. Assuming $1,000 of insurance proceeds, you've got a $400 loss ($1,400 decline in value, less $1,000 of insurance).

Insurance Proceeds	$1,000
Less: Smaller of (1) or (2)	1,400
Gain (Loss)	($ 400)

On the other hand, let's say that the vehicle was worth $6,000 before the casualty, but only $2,100 afterward. Your decline in value would be $3,900 ($6,000, less $2,100). Now your $3,000 adjusted basis is the smaller of the two figures. So, you subtract your insurance recovery from the $3,000 to get the loss deduction. If the insurance company paid $1,000, you'd have a $2,000 loss ($1,000, less $3,000).

Insurance Proceeds	$1,000
Less: Smaller of (1) or (2)	3,000
Gain (Loss)	($2,000)

Appraisals of "before" and "after" values are sometimes difficult to obtain after a casualty. But it is usually necessary to have them when destruction has not been complete. Although they are not complete proof of ownership and value, photographs can certainly help in all stages—appraisal, insurance claim submission, and support of your tax deduction.

If you have never done so, a few hours of photographing and inventorying your business assets could pay big dividends in the event of a theft or casualty. And remember to keep the lists, descriptions, and photographs at a different location. You don't want a fire, storm, theft, or other misfortune to also destroy *them*.

Complete Destruction

When a business asset is stolen or completely destroyed, you figure a loss as if you sold the item for the amount of the insurance proceeds or other recovery you receive. In other words, you subtract its adjusted basis from the cash you get.

For example, assume that the vehicle we have been talking about is completely destroyed in an accident. The adjusted basis to which you had depreciated it was $3,000 ($12,000 cost, less $9,000 of depreciation). If your insurance company pays you $4,500, you've got a $1,500 gain ($4,500 cash, less $3,000). But, if they only give you $2,400, you will have a $600 loss ($2,400 cash, less $3,000).

Insurance Proceeds	$4,500	$2,400
Less: Adjusted Basis	3,000	3,000
Gain (Loss)	$1,500	($ 600)

Losses On Personal-Use Property

Losses on personal-use property, as opposed to business property, are sometimes figured differently from losses on business or investment assets. But they usually *can* be deducted on your tax return.

All losses on personal-use property (your private residence, nonbusiness car, jewelry, and others) are calculated like a partial destruction of business property. Insurance payments are subtracted from the smaller of 1) the decline in fair market value because of the casualty or 2) the cost or other basis of the property. Then $100 is substracted from each loss and 10 percent of your adjusted gross income is subtracted from all losses for the year. (These floors keep small losses off your tax return.)

So, if you have hail damage to your personal residence or find that your nonbusiness car has been stolen, your loss may be calculated differently than the losses found in this chapter—but still deducted.

Important Points

If you have more losses than gains on casualties during a year, your losses can probably be fully deducted from your unprotected ordinary income—profits, dividends, commissions, salary, and others. You may be pleasantly surprised at how much tax they will save.

Too often, people who suffer thefts or casualties either do not remember the details at tax time or are not able to prove the numbers needed to figure losses. These folks suffer two tragedies—one to their property and a second to their tax bills. The first injury may not be avoidable, but the second is.

Since everyone knows that a certain amount of thefts or casualties involving business assets is unavoidable, it makes sense to spend a little time inventorying and photographing property. Valuable assets should be periodically appraised so that—in the event of partial destruction—you'll have a recent estimate of fair market value. These simple precautions can help you make the most of your deductions later on.

Regardless of what type of asset is affected, you can cut the severity of a theft or casualty by using the loss to pay less tax. Uncle Sam wants to share your losses. Why not let him?

4

Tax-Sheltered
Retirement Plans

To get a tax deduction, you must almost always have some type of expense (usually the result of spending cash or incurring a debt). You don't expect any future benefit from the transaction, so you "expense" it, which causes it to be deducted.

But there is one way in which you can generate a deduction simply by investing cash. Rather than giving up cash, you turn it into a different type of asset—one which will continue to work for you for years to come. And, to make matters better, profits these deducted dollars now earn will be sheltered from income taxes until some later date.

How is this possible?

All you have to do is set up a Keogh plan or Individual Retirement Account (IRA) for yourself and make monthly or annual contributions to it.

Evidently, Congress has begun to think that a shift from publi retirement to private retirement should be encouraged in light of the financial difficulties Social Security is facing. Our government also wishes to motivate people to save more of their income.

The result is a gift to the person who works for himself—a gift of potentially large tax savings.

Tax-Free Buildup Is Faster

Each of the dollars of net profits you expose to tax rates is going to have a bite taken out of it. If your marginal (top) tax rate is 40 percent, only 60 cents of each of the last dollars you earn each year will remain in your hands.

By investing 60 cents, you could earn (at a ten percent interest rate) six cents per year. But taxes then take part of this six cents. So, the next year, you're earning on, perhaps, 63 or 64 cents (your original 60 cents, plus three or four cents remaining after taxes hit your six cents of interest).

If you use a Keogh or IRA, your entire dollar (not 60 cents) is invested. This is because taxes do not take any of your annual contribution to the retirement plan. Each whole dollar is lifted cleanly out of your tax return by the act of investing it.

Then, each dollar begins earning interest for you. If you earn ten percent, you receive ten cents for each dollar in your retirement account. And taxes do not take any of this ten cents of earnings. It is completely protected from the tax rates which are applied to your other earnings.

So the next year, you are earning interest on $1.10 (your $1 investment, plus ten cents of earnings), rather than on only 63 or 64 cents.

Each year's contribution repeats this scenario. It is deposited intact, then begins earning tax-free profits to build up your net worth.

You can see how a tax-free investment is able to grow much faster and higher than one which is taxed.

Exactly what should you expect?

If you are able to make the maximum allowable contribution to a Keogh plan for each of 20 consecutive years, and have it grow at a 12 percent compound rate, you'll wind up with over $1 million at the end of that time. If you make the same contributions for 30 years and they grow at a rate of 16 percent through investment in common stock or other inflation-resistant assets, your retirement account will build to about $8 million.

Failing to take advantage of tax-free plans would cause your results to be lower. If you were in the 40 percent tax bracket, you would accumulate about $648,000 (instead of $1 million) or about $4.8 million (instead of $8 million).

The bottom line is that Uncle Sam is leaning over backwards to help you retire in style. All you've got to do is agree to let him help you.

Incorporated or Unincorporated Business

Whether your business is a corporation, partnership, or sole proprietorship, you have access to one or more excellent tax-sheltered retirement plans.

Corporate retirement plans, along with other types of fringe benefits you can get from your own corporation, are discussed in Chapter 11.

This chapter explains the two main types of retirement plans used by people who own sole proprietorships and partnerships. These are Keogh plans and IRA's.

Many banks, savings institutions, mutual funds, money management organizations, stock brokers and others will be happy to help you set up one or both of these plans.

What Keogh Can Do for You

A Keogh plan will allow you to invest (and deduct) up to 15 percent (25 percent in 1984 and later years) of your net profits from self employment. The upper limit on your annual investment/deduction is $15,000 (15 percent of $100,000) in 1983 and $30,000 (25 percent of $120,000) in 1984 and later. If you earn between $750 and $5,000, you can normally contribute/deduct $750. When you earn less than $750, you can use it all.

Let's say that you start your business on a part-time basis in November and earn only $600 before December 31. Since you earn less than $750, you can probably put it all into a Keogh plan and tell Uncle Sam that you did not earn anything.

What if you earned $2,000 in 1983? Fifteen percent of $2,000 is only $300. But the IRS will let you put at least $750 into your plan as long as you earn $750 or more. So, your investment/deduction for the year is $750.

Assume that your net profits are $20,000 in 1983. In this case, 15 percent of $20,000 is $3,000—your contribution for the year.

But when your 1983 profits go over $100,000, your upper limit is still $15,000. You can't say that 15 percent of $300,000 of earnings yields a $45,000 deduction. If you earn $300,000, your maximum investment/deduction for the year is still $15,000.

Annual Profits	$600	$2,000	$20,000	$100,000	$300,000
Investment/ Deduction	$600	$ 750	$ 3,000	$ 15,000	$ 15,000

Watch Your Cost/Benefit Ratio

One drawback of Keogh plans, compared to IRA's, is that you are more likely to find yourself making contributions for your full-time employees.

Let's say that you earn $50,000 and contribute 15 percent of your profits as well as 15 percent of the salaries of three employees. Assuming the employees earned a total of $40,000 during the year, you'd be putting 15 percent of $90,000 (your $50,000, plus their $40,000) into the plan. Your investment/deduction would amount to a total of $13,500. But $6,000 of that (15 percent of $40,000) would belong to your employees—not to you.

	For You	For Them	Total
Profits, Salaries	$50,000	$40,000	$90,000
Contribution From Your Cash	7,500	6,000	13,500

If the $6,000 you are contributing for your employees takes the place of salary you'd otherwise pay them, fine. Otherwise, it is costing you a bundle to build up your retirement fund.

You can see how this would be a serious disadvantage for anyone who has several employees. Of course, there is no disadvantage for someone who is able to operate his business by himself.

If you do have employees and are reluctant to add to your costs by making voluntary contributions for them, you should consider an IRA. Although your maximum contributions allowable to an IRA are less than they would be to a Keogh plan, you won't have to pay for employees' retirements.

Penalties for Withdrawals or Loans

The idea behind tax-sheltered retirement plans is that of postponing the time at which your annual contribution is taxed. Instead of being taxed this year, it goes on your tax return when you withdraw it from the company which handles your Keogh plan or IRA. (Hopefully, this will be during your retirement years when your tax rates are lower.)

So, if you close your Keogh plan and have the cash paid to you, or if you start receiving payments, you will be taxed. If you are in a high tax bracket, the taxes levied by the IRS could be severe.

Similarly, borrowing part or all of your equity in a Keogh plan could lead the IRS to believe that you have received a distribution from your retirement plan. The result is that you will be taxed on the cash when you receive it.

Payout Possibilities

You have already seen how fast a tax-sheltered retirement account can build up if you are making the maximum annual contributions to it. How much will your monthly income be when you stop building it up and start drawing cash out?

There are many forms of annuities which guarantee certain amounts of payments or which will make payments over your statistical lifetime or some other term. But let's assume that you retire at age 60 and simply want your investment paid out to you during the next 25 years.

Assume that you've accumulated $1 million and, while you are drawing equal monthly payments, you leave the remainder invested at 12 percent. Your monthly pension should be in the neighborhood of $10,000.

If you were able to take the path which led you to accumulate $8 million, you would begin drawing equal monthly payments while the remainder continued to earn 16 percent interest. Your monthly pension should amount to around $100,000.

Although the value of the dollar will be less in 20 or 30 years, either of the above figures sounds better than Social Security.

IRA's Are Good, Too

For years, IRA's were available only to people who didn't participate in other retirement plans. Now almost anyone who works can have one.

The maximum annual contribution for an IRA is less than for a Keogh plan. You can contribute/deduct no more than $2,000 per year. If your business profits are less than $2,000 for a year, you can put all of them into an IRA and show zero earnings from the business on your tax return.

If your spouse works, he/she can also invest and deduct all of his/her earnings (up to $2,000 per year) in an IRA. If your spouse does not work, you can invest and deduct another $250 with your own $2,000 (a total of $2,250).

As with Keogh plans, the amount built up in your plan will determine the size of your monthly payments after you retire. Since your maximum annual deductible investment with an IRA is less, you can't expect your potential accumulation to be as great. But companies which are vying for your IRA account seem to think that you can build up over $1 million in 30 to 35 years. If this is the case, your monthly retirement pension could amount to $10,000.

Early withdrawals (except in case of disability) from your IRA can cause income taxes and an additional 10 percent penalty to be assessed on the cash you receive. Tax law wants you to begin receiving payments from your IRA sometime between age 59½ and 70½.

Time for Your Contribution

Tax rules for both Keogh plans and IRA's appear to allow you to make your deductible contribution anytime during and even for a period *after* the year for which you take the deduction. In fact, you can probably make your contribution as late as the due date of your tax return—April 15 of the next year.

In other words, if you want to deduct an annual investment for 19A, you could put cash into the plan as late as April 15, 19B (the next year).

How will this help you save taxes?

You'll be able to determine exactly how much you made for a year and how much taxes the contribution will save you. You will have time to figure out the exact amount you want to put into your Keogh or IRA and will have the opportunity to find enough cash to do it.

Although tax law gives you this extra time to make your annual deposit, it doesn't seem to let you make application for your plan after the end of the year. You will need to take care of that part of this tax break before December 31, even if you wait until after the first of the year to write a check for your contribution.

Important Points

There is little doubt that a retirement plan can grow much faster and larger when it isn't subject to tax than when it is. In these days of inflation, high interest yields, and growth stock opportunities, you may be able to accumulate several million dollars in your retirement plan.

And the annual deductions you can take are very attractive. If your business is small at first, you may be able to put most or all of your profits into a retirement fund and owe absolutely no taxes. As the business grows, you will still be able to contribute and deduct a substantial portion of your profits.

This is one of the few times you'll be able to deduct an investment—an expenditure which leads to an increase in your net worth. Normally, you can deduct only expenses (items which are of no further benefit to your business).

Your annual investment/deduction limit is higher with a Keogh plan than with an IRA. If your profits are high, this alternative may be the best choice.

But, with a Keogh plan, you must cover full-time employees who've been with you for three years or more. If you do not have employees, this won't pose a problem. If you do, this requirement may make a Keogh plan more expensive than it is really worth to you.

An IRA is much more attractive now than it was just a few years ago. The maximum yearly investment allowed is fairly good and the opportunity of having your spouse open another IRA can double your deduction and your tax-free buildup.

Under certain circumstances, it may be possible to open both a Keogh plan and an IRA. When this option is available, your annual deductions and tax-free accumulation can be accelerated further. The institution you choose to administer your plans can tell you whether or not you are eligible for this double benefit.

Self-employed retirement plans are well worth your consideration. Retirement may seem to be a long distance away. But even if you're not currently thinking ahead to retirement, these deductions and tax-free increases in your net worth can make a Keogh plan or IRA an attractive part of your overall tax-saving effort.

5

Checklist of
Business Deductions

Each spring, newspapers and magazines are full of little articles about which items of expense are tax deductible. These news stories are aimed almost exclusively at the individual who has never considered going into business for himself. Consequently, they don't offer much in the way of tax savings.

Many more deductions are offered to businesses than individuals can use on their nonbusiness returns. They are so numerous, in fact, that it's easy to overlook several of them.

This chapter alphabetically lists the most common business deductions which can be used in sole proprietorships, partnerships, and corporations. Since the list is so lengthy, only a brief explanation is given for each deduction—enough so that you will keep careful records and receipts when you encounter it.

Other chapters single out several of the more complex deductions and give additional information on each.

Accident and Health Insurance

Premiums you pay for accident and health insurance for your employees are normally deductible. Those you pay for yourself can be taken as an itemized (personal) deduction if you own a sole proprietorship or partnership. They may be a business deduction when paid through your own corporation as a fringe benefit to you (Chapter 11).

Accounting Fees

Amounts you pay to accountants for bookkeeping, financial statement and tax return preparation, advice, audits, and other help can be deducted.

Advertising

The costs you incur to advertise your products or services are deductible. These may include amounts you pay for newspaper, magazine, television, radio, billboard, and other types of advertising.

Amortization

Intangible assets, such as copyrights, patents, trademarks, and organization costs, are amortized like plant and equipment are depreciated. Amortization expense should be listed as a business expense on your tax return.

Appraisals

When you refinance property or apply for other types of business loans, it may be necessary for you to obtain an appraisal of certain business assets. Except when they are related to the acquisition of property, appraisals are usually deductible.

Automobile Expenses

If you use a car or truck in your business, you can figure your deduction for it with either the mileage method or the depreciation plus actual costs method. In most cases, your deduction will be larger in the first few years with the depreciation plus actual costs method (Chapter 1).

Bad Debts Expense

When you sell merchandise or services on credit, you will occasionally fail to collect an account or note receivable from a customer. If you are using the accrual basis of accounting (Chapter 7), you may wish to deduct bad debts as you discover that they can't be collected or you may choose to deduct an estimate of uncollectible accounts at the end of each year.

Capital Losses

Subject to annual limits, losses on sales of capital assets can be deducted against your capital gains or ordinary income (such as salary, commissions, interest, and dividends). The ways in which an individual can benefit most from capital losses are explained in Chapter 19. If your corporation sells a capital asset at a loss, the result can be used only to offset a capital gain (Chapter 20).

Casualty Insurance

Premiums for insuring your business property from casualties are deductible.

Casualty Losses

When a sudden, unexpected, unusual event (such as a storm or accident) causes damage to your property, you may have a deductible loss. Chapter 3 shows you how to calculate your loss.

Charitable Contributions

Cash or property you donate to a qualified charity may be a personal deduction (when made through your sole proprietorship or partnership) or a business deduction (through your corporation).

Commissions

When you pay a commission for the sale of an asset, you will subtract the commissions for buying and selling the item from your sales price.

Conventions

The costs of attending business conventions (meals, lodging, transportation, fees, and others) can be deducted. When you combine attendance at a convention with a pleasure trip, especially in a foreign country, your deduction can be severely limited. Be certain that your expenses for conventions are well-documented. If your return is audited (Chapter 24), this is one item which you see questioned.

Cost of Goods Sold

If your business sells merchandise, the cost of what you sell each year is a deduction. In fact, this is the largest deduction many businesses place on their returns. Your choice of inventory method (Chapter 8) can substantially affect the size of this deduction.

Depletion

If you mine minerals or otherwise harvest natural resources (or allow them to be taken from your property), you may qualify for generous depletion deductions. Depletion can be taken on such diverse products as timber, sand, coal, and oil.

Depreciation

Possibly the deduction which can save you more taxes than any other, depreciation can be taken liberally on buildings (Chapter 13) and on vehicles, equipment, furnishings, and other property (Chapter 15). The result of using depreciation properly can be a large interest-free loan from Uncle Sam.

Dues

Annual dues you pay for your memberships in business and professional organizations are a reasonable cost of doing business. Since you may receive bills for annual membership fees for some business organizations at your home, remember to carefully search both your business *and* personal check books when you are adding up this deduction.

Education

Costs of courses and seminars which improve your abilities to do well in your business are normally deductible. Your expenses can include books, tuition, supplies, transportation, and (if the course or seminar is out of town) meals and lodging. Chapter 1 goes into more detail about transportation, meals, and lodging.

Efficiency Studies

Amounts you pay to consultants to improve the efficiency of your business may be deducted.

Employees' Business-Related Expenses

When employees pay expenses (which appear in this chapter) for your business, your reimbursement of them will normally be deductible. Be certain that your employees give you a written accounting of the costs for which you repay them so that the documentation for your tax return will be adequate.

Entertainment

Most entertainment for which you pay to improve your business can be deducted (Chapter 1).

Excise Taxes

Excise taxes on items you purchase for business use are deductible.

Gasoline and Oil

Using the depreciation plus actual costs method of figuring your auto or truck deduction allows you to place your expenditures for gasoline and oil on your tax return. If you use the mileage allowance method for calculating your auto or truck deduction, the cost of gasoline and oil is already included in the amount the IRS allows for each mile driven. So, using this method prevents you from deducting the actual amounts you spend for gasoline and oil. Chapter 1 gives you additional information on this deduction.

Gifts

Gifts both to customers and to employees can be deducted (Chapter 1). Be very careful to watch your limits on each type. Normally, gifts to each customer should not exceed $25 per year. Gifts to employees for safety, longevity, or productivity can go as high as $1,600 as long as the average cost is no more than $400.

Interest

Interest you pay for business or investment purposes is deductible. Remember that paying more than $10,000 annually for interest to carry investments could cause part of your deduction to be postponed (Chapter 22).

Janitorial Services

This item would include the costs of having your business premises regularly cleaned.

Legal Fees

Amounts you spend for legal services related to your business can be deducted.

Liability Insurance

The costs of insuring your business and business property from legal actions for injury to others is a deduction.

Licenses

Your business may be required to obtain annual licenses from state, local, or federal authorities. The cost of these is a normal business expense.

Life Insurance Premiums

Your business can usually deduct premiums it pays for life insurance on employees' lives where their families are the beneficiaries. If the insurance is of the "whole life" type, premiums are taxed to employees as if they were extra salary. However, premiums on group term life insurance up to a policy amount of $50,000 may be deductible by you, but not taxed to employees (Chapter 11). You may even consider yourself an employee of your own corporation for this purpose.

Lodging

When you are out of town on business, the cost of your lodging is an allowable business expense (Chapter 1).

Losses

In addition to casualty losses, your business may experience a loss by selling an item for less than your cost or adjusted basis. Such losses are normally deductible, offsetting part of your business income. Great care must be taken if you wish to take maximum advantage of capital losses (Chapters 19 and 20).

Meals

Food and beverages you purchase for employees are normally deductible. They can also be used on your tax return if they're entertainment or if your corporation can reasonably require you to eat on the business premises (Chapter 11). Meals purchased while you are out of town on business are often deductible (Chapter 1).

Moving Expenses

Even if you are self-employed, moving expenses can be deducted when you meet two tests: 1) your new place of business must be at least 35 miles farther from your home than was your old place of business; and 2) you must work in the new area for at least 78 weeks out of the first two years after you move.

Net Operating Losses

If your business has a loss from operations, you may be able to carry it back to prior years as a deduction against earlier income or forward to future years as an offset against future earnings. When your business is a sole proprietorship, partnership, or Subchapter S corporation, you can use an operating loss as a deduction against your income from other sources. If your business is a regular corporation, business losses can be used only to offset corporate income in other years (Chapter 9).

Office Supplies

The cost of office supplies you use during the year is a business expense for your tax return.

Painting

When painting takes the form of an ordinary repair, it is deductible. If it is part of an overall effort to extend an asset's life, it may not be.

Parking

Don't forget to deduct your business parking charges. If you do not receive a receipt or cancelled check for this item, record it in your expense diary.

Points

Except when they compensate a lender for specific services, such as appraisals or the preparation of loan documents, points are considered a deductible interest expense.

Postage

Your business postage expense for the year can be deducted. If you do not write checks for postage, always ask for a receipt from the clerk who assists you at the post office.

Post Office Box Rent

The rent for a post office box in which to receive your business mail is deductible.

Prepayment Penalties

Prepayment penalties on long-term loans are often deducted as interest.

Printing

Printing costs may become an asset if you have a large quantity of items produced for your business. When they are sold or used up, these products become an expense for your tax return.

Promotion

Costs of publicizing and promoting your business and its products are usually deductible.

Property Taxes

State and local property taxes on your business assets are a reasonable business expense.

Rent

If you prefer to rent, rather than buy, buildings and/or equipment you need for your business, rental payments are normally deductible.

Repairs

Repairs of business assets can be deducted. But you must carefully distinguish between repairs and "betterments" or "improvements" which lengthen an asset's life or make it work better. These latter expenditures must be depreciated (deducted over several years, rather than in the year you make them).

Retirement Plan Contributions

Your investments in IRA and Keogh plans, with limits, are deductible (Chapter 4). Likewise, your corporation's contribution for you to a corporate retirement plan is deductible up to an annual limit (Chapter 11).

Research and Development Expenditures

Although you may be limited in the annual amount of it you can deduct, research and development expenditures can be a valuable source of tax savings to a technically-oriented business.

Safe Deposit Box Rental

Rent for the safe deposit box you use to store your valuable business papers and documents can be deducted.

Salaries and Wages

The compensation of employees is a business deduction. Your own salary can be deducted only when you are an employee of your own corporation (Chapter 9).

Security Services

It is increasingly necessary to hire either daytime or night security services for businesses. These costs are normal business expenses.

Shipping

Amounts you pay for shipping your products to customers make up your "Shipping Expense" deduction.

Social Security

The social security taxes you must pay to match the amounts you withhold from employees' salaries and wages are deductible.

Sports Equipment

When bought for business publicity, sports equipment can become a cost similar to advertising or promotion.

Storm Damage

Storm damage may be deducted as a casualty loss under most circumstances (Chapter 3).

Subscriptions

Amounts you spend each year for subscriptions to newspapers and magazines which enable you to better run your business are normally deductible. If you stray from the area of professional or business publications, you may invite argument from the IRS.

Tax Advice and Return Preparation

Like accounting and legal fees, your business tax advice and return preparation are deductible.

Telephone Expense

Both local and long-distance business telephone service can be deducted. If you own your telephone equipment, be sure to deduct depreciation expense on it (Chapter 15) and to take investment tax credit on it in the year you buy it (Chapter 16). Using your home phone for both business and personal use normally calls for a division of costs between deductible business amounts and nondeductible personal charges.

Theft Losses

The loss of business property through theft may result in a business deduction (Chapter 3).

Tolls

Tolls paid during business travel become a business expense.

Tools

If tools you buy for your business have an estimated life of less than one year, they can often be deducted in the year you buy them. When determining the length of their life, be sure to consider such factors as breakage and theft.

Transportation Costs

Costs of local and out-of-town business transportation (except commuting from your home to the office) may be deducted. If you use your own vehicle, you can choose either the mileage method or the depreciation plus actual costs method of figuring your deduction (Chapter 1). When using public transportation, such as airlines or trains, the actual cost of your ticket is deductible.

Traveling Expenses

Meals, lodging, and transportation for business trips are deductible items (Chapter 1).

Unemployment Insurance

The cost of unemployment insurance you pay on behalf of your employees is a normal business expense.

Utilities

You can deduct utilities (gas, water, electricity, garbage collection, and others) for your business.

Worthless Securities

When an investment you make in stock becomes absolutely worthless, it is considered to be a capital loss on the last day of the year in which it becomes worthless. If you own shares of stock in companies which now have questionable financial standings, you should review the status of each near the end of the year.

Important Points

No list of deductions can hope to be complete. Each business has expenses which are peculiar to its industry or method of operation. One of your best bets for finding every possible deduction is to go through your cancelled checks for the last couple of years. Add any additional items you find to the list presented above.

Discovering deductions you might otherwise miss is like finding cash. Each allowable deduction will save taxes on your return. The cash saved can then be reinvested in your business or used for any purpose you choose.

Some of the items listed above are deductible under certain circumstances, but not under others. When in doubt, try to spend your money so that you generate the maximum deduction for your dollar. Several chapters in this book explain how this can be done in different cases. For example, Chapter 1 shows precisely when the cost of meals and lodging can and can't be placed on your tax return.

The year in which you deduct several of the items on this list may depend upon whether you are using the cash or accrual method of accounting. Roughly, the cash method would recognize an expense when you write and send a check. The accrual method records an expense when it is incurred, owed, or used up. Chapter 7 gives more detail about each method of accounting and its advantages and drawbacks.

Whether an item is deductible this year or next—or across several years—it is important that you remember to use it to save taxes. Part of your year-end tax planning strategy (Chapter 7) should be to make sure that you take every deduction available to you and that you make use of it as soon as legally possible.

Uncle Sam deliberately filled tax law with countless business deductions. Using as many of them as you can to save your tax dollars is as much a part of building your business capital as is generating additional sales.

PART TWO

Tax Tricks for Businesses Only

6

Splitting Income Among Family Members for Lower Taxes

Tax rates in this country move progressively higher as a person's income increases. If you're in the higher tax brackets, federal income taxes can take half of each additional dollar you earn. State and local taxes can make the burden even more severe.

The income of many businesses can be split among family members so that no one individual is placed in those higher tax brackets. The splitting can actually result in lower overall taxes on the total profits of the enterprise. More profits are available for reinvestment.

Any business which is to have its earnings divided must usually be one which earns a good part of its profits from the capital invested in it. For example, if you have $150,000 invested in your business and earn $125,000 per year from it, part of the profit may be due to your efforts. But part is also earned by your capital investment. So, the $125,000 of income can be allocated among family members in order to lower taxes.

On the other hand, a lawyer or doctor receives almost all of his income from his own labor. When an individual such as this earns virtually all of his income from personal effort, any attempt on his part to say that others (wife, parents, children) earned part of it could be met with strong objections from the IRS.

How To Split Your Business

With such big tax savings at stake, tax law figures it can make some hefty demands. In order to split business income, you must actually transfer part of the ownership of your business to others. You must also give to the recipients the voice in management which their new ownership percentages justify.

This sounds like an awfully big step, doesn't it? But before you let those two requirements stop you from reading the rest of this chapter, let's bring out all the problems they could raise and discuss them objectively.

First of all, ask yourself what may be an unpleasant question at this point: Who will get my business when I retire or die?

Some or all of these folks are probably the same people who should share the taxes (and income) on it while you are still strongly participating in management.

Of course, this may be where any discussion of splitting profit ends. Any number of events may already have happened or be likely to occur which would make you unwilling to give up one iota of ownership or management authority. If so, this method for lowering taxes on your business is not for you.

But let us look at the possibilities anyway. Assume that you've settled on your son and daughter as the persons who will eventually get your business. If they are both upstanding types who are interested in the business, good luck. But what is the likelihood of unpleasant management confrontations with your son or daughter? Is there a chance they will lose or sell their ownership interests to outsiders?

Let's not kid ourselves. These are real possibilities. Your son may become a dropout from society, squandering his savings and objecting to your "capitalist" principles. Your daughter may marry a freeloader who is determined to make you miserable.

Obviously, life carries no guarantees. Nothing these days seems to be stable. All we can do is look at the possibilities and decide for ourselves whether or not each choice outweighs the alternatives.

Stand back and ask yourself if you'll really mind your dropout son receiving part of the income to lower your taxes. He might have the right to participate in decisions about the firm but have no desire to do so.

After your daughter marries, will your son-in-law actually want to play a part in the business? If they divorce, will he be able to take part of the ownership with him, or can the transfer of part of the business be structured so that it remains your daughter's separate property?

Other arrangements may be more attractive. If you split the business with your elderly parents who have no interest in playing a management role, you may admirably achieve your goal of cutting taxes. When you split income with children who are too young to be interested in the business, or who have other interests, you win again. If you have two children who are following you into the business, and another who is going through a difficult stage, you could leave out the third until he becomes more stable.

Do not discard the idea of splitting income merely because of potential family problems. You and your attorney may be able to structure the entire deal so that your risks are minimized. The point of the whole process is that you must be comfortable with the new relationships that are established or that the reduction of taxes at least outweighs any possible discomfort.

Salaries May Be a Good Compromise

If, at this point, there simply are not any situations where you'd be comfortable giving up part of your ownership and management, you can still achieve basically the same result by hiring your children or others and paying them salaries. These salaries would reduce your business profits because they would be deducted like any other expenses. Your children or other relatives would report part of the business' profits and pay part of the taxes you used to show on your tax return.

Although paying salaries allows you to retain ownership and control, the people who receive salaries actually have to work for what you pay them. By owning part of the business, your daughter might have been able to stay at home and still help you cut your taxes. But as an employee, she'll have to spend time at the office just like everybody else.

Splitting Different Types of Organizations

We've seen so far that 1) income can be split only when capital is an income-producing factor in the business and 2) ownership interests in the business must actually be transferred to each of those who will be taxed on the income.

If you have decided to split your business, you must be careful how you do it. Selling or giving ownership interests to others can sometimes cause a surprise tax bill for *you*.

Sole Proprietorship

A sole proprietorship, by definition, is owned by one person. When you sell or give part of the business to someone else, you're creating a partnership. You must watch out for taxes in several places.

1) If you give part of the business to relatives, you may have to pay gift taxes. The gift tax is a "progressive" tax, like the income tax, which amounts to more on larger gifts than on smaller ones. Normally, you can give up to $10,000 worth of gifts ($20,000 if you and your spouse own them jointly) to any one person per year without having to pay any gift taxes.

2) If your business has certain unusual types of assets (e.g., notes on installment sales you've made) you might have some income taxes as a result of the gift.

3) If you sell part of the business to relatives, you may have to pay income taxes this year on the difference between what the relatives pay you and your cost or other basis in the part of the business sold.

Partnership

If the business is already a partnership and you split your interest in the enterprise with a relative or relatives, some of the same problems may arise.

1) If you give them part of your ownership interest in the business, you could owe gift taxes. And, in a few situations, some income taxes might also result in the year of the gift.

2) Selling part of your interest could cause a taxable gain on the difference between what they pay you and your cost or other basis in your partnership interest.

One other problem can arise if half or more of the total ownership of a partnership is sold within a 12-month period. When this happens, tax law terminates the partnership. All income from the beginning of the year up to that point is taxed. So, be very careful about selling half or more of a partnership.

Corporation

Splitting your corporation may be less messy tax-wise than dividing a sole proprietorship or partnership. All you have to do is give or sell shares of stock to the relatives with whom you wish to split income.

1) Giving shares of stock could cause gift taxes to arise when their value is over the $10,000 (or $20,000 if owned jointly) annual limit per recipient.

2) Selling shares of stock will cause income taxes on the difference between what they pay you and your cost or other basis.

A Subchapter S corporation (Chapter 12) is ideal for this type of splitting. The income of the business is allocated to those who own shares on the last day of the corporation's tax year. Each owner's share of the income goes to his own personal tax return and is taxed to him instead of to the corporation. It may be well worth your while to incorporate a business and to get Subchapter S tax status before splitting it.

Regardless of whether you are splitting a sole proprietorship, partnership, or corporation, be sure that the transfer of ownership to others is an *actual* transfer and that the recipients have an appropriate voice in management. Otherwise, the "split" probably won't work. All income will still be taxed to you.

Whichever way you choose, it is a good idea (as in all major transactions) to have your tax advisor look at all angles before you do it. He may be able to save you thousands of dollars in taxes with a very simple change in the way you go about the split.

Cutting Your Total Taxes

Although income splitting can work at almost any level of earnings, let's take an extreme example to illustrate dramatically the advantages a business owner could receive. Assume that you earn $500,000 annually from a chain of dry cleaning establishments and that you lose $230,000 of your profits as income taxes. The remaining $270,000 goes for your current living expenses and reinvestment in the business.

Let's say that you decide to split the business with your three children, keeping two-fifths of the ownership, and giving each of them one-fifth. Your personal taxes afterward may be, perhaps, $80,000 out of a $200,000 income. The children might each earn $100,000 and pay taxes of around $30,000.

After the split, the overall tax bill is $170,000 (your $80,000 plus $30,000 for each of the three children). This is $60,000 less than your taxes were before the split.

Your personal income after taxes is now $150,000 less. (You were keeping $270,000 before, but now you have only $120,000 left after taxes.) Your children, however, now each have $70,000 after taxes, for a total of $210,000. Thus, the overall family income after taxes is now $330,000 (your $120,000 plus their $210,000), instead of only $270,000. Splitting the ownership of your business has kept $60,000 in the family which would have otherwise been taken as taxes.

	Before Split	After Split
Earnings		
Your share	$500,000	$200,000
Your children's share	-0-	300,000
Total Earnings	$500,000	$500,000
Taxes		
Your share	$230,000	$ 80,000
Your children's share	-0-	90,000
Total Taxes	$230,000	$170,000
After-Tax Earnings		
Your share	$270,000	$120,000
Your children's share	-0-	210,000
Total After-Tax Earnings	$270,000	$330,000

You may not feel as though you can give up the $150,000 by which your take-home pay dropped or that you can yield absolute management of the business. On the other hand, by giving up $150,000 and part of your say in company matters, you have increased your children's incomes by $210,000—$60,000 of it at the expense of the IRS. That is a nice trick, for sure.

The potential savings in taxes year after year from now until the time that you had planned to give them the business or that they would have inherited it anyway can be substantial. Even though your personal income is less, and even though you may not really feel like sharing decision-making responsibilities, your satisfaction at seeing tax dollars turned into family wealth can be fine compensation.

Whether or not splitting of income with family members will work in your case can only be decided by weighing all the possibilities. You must determine whether or not the potential tax savings and satisfaction across the coming years will offset any probable disadvantages.

How Income Is Split

Even after ownership transfers are made, the IRS wants to make sure that you, the original owner, are taxed on the income you actually earn. They first want you to show a salary for yourself which is commensurate with the work you put into the business after the split. Then it is usually advisable to divide profits remaining after salaries in the approximate ownership ratios.

In the prior example, you retained two-fifths of the ownership of the dry cleaning business. If you devoted little time to the concern after its division, letting your children run it, you might not earn any salary. You might wind up with no more (perhaps less) than two-fifths of the total business profits.

On the other hand, if you continued to devote your full time to the enterprise, tax law says that you should give yourself a reasonable compensation before any split of the remaining profits go to capital interests in the business.

Let's say that your effort for the year was worth $100,000. Of the $500,000 total earnings, you would get the first $100,000. If your children gave no effort to the business (and earned no salaries), the remaining $400,000 would most likely be divided in the ownership ratios. You would get two-fifths, or $160,000, and the children would receive the remainder.

You'd be personally taxed, then, on a total of $260,000— $100,000 of reasonable compensation for your work during the year, and $160,000 return on your capital. If the children received no salaries, they would be taxed only on the remaining $240,000.

Formal Agreements

When you split a Subchapter S corporation, you do not need an agreement about how profits will be divided. After salaries are paid, the remainder will go to each person in the fraction of the enterprise he owns. If you own 45 percent of the stock, you'll probably get 45 percent of the profits after salaries.

The earnings of a regular corporation are taxed to itself (Chapter 9), then any dividends paid to owners are taxed again to them. Dividends are normally paid out to you on the basis of the number of shares you own.

But, if you divide a partnership or sole proprietorship among relatives, you'll want a carefully-drawn partnership agreement which spells out profit- and loss-sharing percentages. This is because profits and losses may be divided in different ratios from each other and in different ratios than partners' capital.

For example, you might be in a high tax bracket and prefer to have income taxed to other people, but want as much loss as possible for your own tax return. If you own one-third of the capital of a partnership, you might agree to accept one-fourth of any profits and one-half of any losses. As long as the IRS did not think you were going against "economic reality," you could divide profits and losses by the agreement.

If you don't have a written and reasonable partnership agreement, the IRS may just assign salaries to owners and split remaining income or loss by each person's ownership percentage. So, if you own one-third of the business, you will get one-third of the profits or losses.

Important Points

If the earnings of your business are not generated solely by your efforts, income-splitting among family members may reduce the overall tax bill. This can be true whether the earnings are as high as in the examples used in this chapter or much lower.

Since you must transfer ownership interests and offer some decision-making ability to others, you need to carefully consider all sides of such a transfer, including the "human" factors. You may choose to make certain transfers now, and others later. That way, your tax bill would be reduced to some extent immediately and further at some later date.

Your after-tax income will probably decrease as a result of splitting your income with others, but the savings in taxes could allow relatives to benefit far more than the amount by which your personal earnings decline. One possible disadvantage can be the taxes which arise when you transfer ownership interests to others. If you sell, even to your children, you could owe some income taxes on the sale. When you give away valuable portions of a business, gift taxes can arise. But taking maximum advantage of the $10,000 ($20,000 if the business is owned jointly with your spouse) annual gift tax exclusion over a period of years will reduce the tax bite.

Splitting your income and business *can* lead to potential problems with your children or other relatives. In some cases, just the idea of these difficulties is enough to prevent you from using this tax break. On the other hand, satisfaction from seeing overall family after-tax income rise dramatically and your current enjoyment of the success of your children or other relatives are strong arguments for splitting income among family members.

7

Choosing the Accounting Method to Postpone Taxes

There are two basic methods of keeping books for your business—the cash method and the accrual method. The size of your business or other factors may dictate which is chosen. But the cash method can allow most organizations more flexibility in deciding which revenues and expenses will reach the tax return in a specific year.

The cash method says that revenue should be placed on your tax return when you receive cash and that expense should be shown when you write and send a check. This is the simplest method of accounting and, due to the relatively inexpensive way in which it can be used, is employed widely in smaller businesses.

The accrual method says that revenue must go to your tax return when you "earn" it, regardless of when cash is received. Thus, if you sell a product or service to someone, it is revenue when you deliver or provide it, not when cash reaches you.

Likewise, an expense is shown under the accrual method when it is "incurred," "owed," or "used," not when cash is paid. You record the cost of a product or service as "expense" for your business when it has no further use, not when you pay for it. For example, let's say that you pay in advance for something that will last for some period of time, such as insurance. You show it as an expense when it is used up, not when you pay for it. If people work for you in December, you show their labor as an expense in December—even though you may pay them in January (*after* you record the expense).

Tax law requires (with few exceptions) that a business which manufactures or buys and sells merchandise use the accrual method for its sales and purchases of merchandise. This means that sales must be shown in the year they're made, regardless of when cash is received. Likewise, inventory bought can only be shown as an expense in the year it is sold, not when it's purchased. On the other hand, such a business can normally use the cash method for all its other transactions, such as salaries, interest, advertising, and other expenses, deducting them when paid.

A service business, which doesn't receive much revenue from the sale of merchandise, can choose to use the cash method on almost all of its activities. A barber, for example, can show hair cutting revenue on his tax return when he receives cash, and advertising expense when he pays cash. The time that the hair is cut or the benefit is received from advertising is not important to a business which uses the cash method. The inflow and outflow of cash are.

Who Uses the Cash Method?

Smaller businesses, especially service companies, tend to use the cash method of recording revenues and expenses. It is easier and faster to use than the accrual method. So, bookkeeping costs are less. Bookkeeping can normally be accomplished by looking at the deposits and payments shown in your bank statement. Typically, a person with little or no bookkeeping background can be quickly taught to prepare basic accounting records under the cash method.

Unfortunately, this method doesn't produce financial statements as accurate as those given by the accrual method. Instead of showing revenues when earned and expenses when incurred or owed, revenues are recorded in the year cash is received (regardless of when earned). Expenses are recognized when cash is paid (not when owed).

Neither does the cash basis produce financial statements for which a Certified Public Accountant can give an unqualified opinion. Although bankers, prospective investors, and others may happily rely on statements produced under the cash method, those statements can never carry the ultimate assurance of a Certified Public Accountant's opinion.

For most small firms, the lower costs of bookkeeping far outweigh the disadvantages of the cash method. As an enterprise becomes larger, accuracy becomes more important to lenders and others.

Who Uses the Accrual Method?

Income statements and balance sheets are usually more accurate when the accrual method is used than when the cash method is employed. Inflows and outflows of cash (particularly when a business is granting credit to others and receiving it from suppliers) have little to do with actual accounting revenue and expense numbers.

Medium-sized and larger organizations often have their own expert accounting staffs who are familiar with the accrual method of reporting revenues and expenses. They can usually maintain these records much more easily than can a smaller business.

The accrual method probably allows less flexibility in tax planning. But many of these larger companies can't move as quickly to carry out tax plans as can a small one anyway. So, the increased flexibility of the cash method would be of little use to them. Another fact which prevents them from using the cash method is that these businesses normally cannot approach their lenders without a Certified Public Accountant's opinion (which means using the accrual method).

Advantages of the Cash Method

One major reason why you might prefer the cash method is the fact that you can often pay and deduct certain expenses in one year, even though they may be used up in later years. For example, if you pay advertising or promotion costs in 19A for advertisements which will appear in 19B, you can deduct those expenses (within reason) in 19A.

Since you would deduct the costs sooner or later anyway, this technique may not reduce your taxes in total over a period of years. But it allows you to pay them *later*. Paying taxes later, rather than sooner, means that you receive the closest thing there is to an interest-free loan from the IRS.

Another big reason to use the cash basis is that you can be paid and taxed next year for services you provide this year. Have you ever wondered why your doctor waits so long to bill you for that November visit? One reason may be that he wants the revenue to be taxed in the next year.

Using the cash method means that you can benefit from carefully examining your tax situation near the end of the year. When you want to postpone taxes, pay in December those expenses which will be due early in the next year.

If you have a service business, plan the collection of cash for work already done so that it reaches you in January of the next year, rather than December of the current year. This will place it on next year's tax return.

If you own a business which primarily sells merchandise, you must show sales revenue and cost-of-merchandise-sold expense in the year a sale actually occurs, regardless of inflows and outflows of cash. But other items may usually be shown on the tax return when cash is received or sent.

Certain expenses have been abused by cash method firms to the point where the IRS may ask that they be moved to the year they are actually owed or used, rather than when paid. Interest and rent, for instance, have too often been paid and deducted in one year, even though they were not due until the next year or later. The government may now force you to deduct these in the year they are owed, rather than allowing a deduction for the year of payment—even though your business uses the cash method.

Similarly, if you pay insurance which covers more than one year of future protection, the government may allow you to deduct the expenditure only as the insurance expires, not in the year of the payment.

You may *not* be forced to deduct any of these expenses in years other than when you pay them, but the likelihood is greater for them than for others.

There are exceptions, but proper management of cash receipts and disbursements for a cash method business can usually postpone taxes until a later year.

Advantages of the Accrual Method

Although it lacks the flexibility of the cash method, the accrual method does allow the advantage of deducting expenses before you pay them. This comes in handy when you are short of cash at the end of a year but need tax deductions. Under the cash method, you would have to pay cash to get a deduction. With the accrual method, you can incur and deduct an expense now, but pay later.

Let's say, for example, that you need deductions in 19A, but have no cash. As an accrual method business owner, you could deduct labor, maintenance, consulting fees, and many other items which you have used and owe, even though you won't pay for them until 19B. If you operated under the cash method, they would be deductible only when paid (19B).

This may not be the advantage it seems. Although he cannot take a deduction for *un*paid expenses which he owes, a cash method business owner can borrow cash from a bank and take deductions as he uses the funds to pay expenses. The year in which the loan is repaid is irrelevant.

For example, if labor is $1,000, maintenance is $500, and consulting fees are $3,000 in 19A, the accrual basis business can probably take the deductions in 19A—whether paid or not. But the cash method business also receives the deductions in 19A if it *pays* for them in 19A, even if it borrows from a bank to do so.

Rent Revenue Received in Advance

The accrual method has disappointing results if a business, as landlord, ever collects rent in advance from tenants. Ordinarily, income is taxed when earned, regardless of when received. Rent received in advance, however, is taxed when you get it under both the cash and accrual methods.

This can compound problems when you try to offset rental income by using the cash for deductions. Regardless of when the accrual method business owner pays them, his expenses are not deductible until they are actually owed or used up. If he pays them in advance with rent received in advance (or with any other funds), he doesn't have a deduction until the year they are actually owed or no longer of benefit to the business.

For example, a payment in advance, by an accrual method business, for advertising or insurance does not generate a deduction. The deduction is allowed only as the advertising or insurance is *used* by the company.

On the other hand, a cash method enterprise which receives rent in advance can then pay various expense items in advance and take deductions for most or all of them.

Year-End Tax Moves That Help

Part of your strategy to save taxes should be to review your business' tax situation near the end of each year. Normally, you'll want to do everything you can to increase expenses as much as possible and postpone income. Some tax-saving techniques work for either the cash or accrual method. Others are appropriate for only one of the two.

Cash or Accrual Method

The following year-end tax moves work whether you're using the cash method *or* the accrual method.

1) Switch to LIFO inventory (Chapter 8) so that your Cost of Goods Sold deduction is higher.

2) If you have obsolete or damaged inventory, sell it or give it

away so that you can take your loss on it in this year's tax return.

3) If you receive merchandise near the end of the year and include it in your count of ending inventory, be certain that it is included in your Purchases account for the year. Otherwise, your Cost of Goods Sold deduction will be smaller than you deserve.

4) If your business is not a corporation, consider selling a limited amount of capital assets which are worth less than what you paid for them. The losses can cut your income (Chapter 19) and you can use the cash to generate additional deductions in other areas.

5) Sell additional capital assets, as needed, to wipe out capital gains or "soak up" capital losses (Chapters 19 and 20).

6) If you've got equipment which is nearly worthless, sell or abandon it so that you can take a loss on it this year.

7) If you are planning to buy additional equipment early next year, do it this year instead. The investment credit (Chapter 16) and depreciation (Chapter 15) will cut your taxes earlier.

8) Make needed repairs this year, rather than next. (If you're using the cash method of accounting, remember to pay for them this year.)

9) Ship products you are selling on an F.O.B. destination basis. Title won't pass to the buyer until they are delivered (early next year), so the shipment goes into *next* year's sales.

10) Make year-end sales on approval or on consignment so they'll be recorded as revenue next year.

11) If you get orders near the end of the year, do not ship them or send invoices until early the next year.

12) In order to postpone income until later years, begin selling your merchandise with the installment method (Chapter 21).

13) If your business isn't a corporation, start a Keogh or IRA (Chapter 4) and make contributions to it.

14) If you own a corporation, make contributions to your corporate retirement plan (Chapter 11).

15) Make next year's charitable contributions this year (but stay under annual limits on such gifts).

Accrual Method Only

Some tax-saving actions are appropriate only if your business operates under the accrual method.

1) Even if you won't have the cash to pay for them until next year, incur deductible expenses (repairs, promotion, advertising, consulting, *et al*) this year.

2) Declare bonuses to employees this year, even if you pay them next year. (If the business is a corporation and recipients own more than 50 percent of the stock, you'll have to pay their bonuses within two and one-half months of the year end.)

3) Accrue vacation pay for employees and deduct it.

4) Avoid accepting prepaid rent until next year.

5) If you are using the "reserve" method for recording your Bad Debts deduction, make as large an addition to the reserve as you can justify.

6) If you do not use the "reserve" method for Bad Debts, write off all debts which you probably won't collect. Later collection means that they will be added back to income—but probably in the year of collection.

Cash Method Only

Cash method businesses also get their share of tax breaks which are not available to accrual basis enterprises.

1) Delay billing customers for services performed so that cash won't come in (and be taxed) until next year.

2) Prepay selected expenses (other than rent, interest, or insurance) so that they'll go into your tax return this year.

3) Pay bills you already owe this year so that you can put the deductions on your current tax return.

4) If you need to borrow cash to pay or prepay expenses, consider doing so. This can help you generate deductions *now*. The year you repay the loan does not have any effect on when you get your deductions.

5) Buy supplies you'll need early next year so that you can deduct them this year.

6) If you have a choice between paying property taxes late this year or early next year, pay them this year.

If You Own Two Businesses

One possible source of relief for the person who owns two or more separate businesses is that each enterprise can use a different tax method. If one is on the accrual method, others can use the accrual method *or* the cash method. When one unincorporated business gets locked into an insoluble tax problem at the end of the year, quick action to build a tax loss for another business can provide relief.

Let's say that you own an accrual method furniture store and several cash method real estate rental properties. You might run into a problem with too much income and too few deductions if your furniture store has a good year. But you could then turn to your rental properties for additional tax deductions in the current year. You could use any of the year-end moves already explained. Expenses which could be paid early or additional depreciation, for example, might help you out.

Important Points

Which method is better for your business—the cash method or the accrual method?

The answer to that question depends on how large your business is, how fast you can react to tax planning, and whether or not you need a Certified Public Accountant's opinion on your financial statements for banking or other purposes.

If you have a small company which can turn on a dime, wish to save money on bookkeeping and accounting costs, need only informal statements for your banker, and wish to get the largest possible interest-free loan from the IRS, the cash method is probably for you.

Although it will normally be required to use the accrual method for its sales and cost of goods sold (i.e., show revenues and cost of sales in the tax return for the actual year of sale, rather than the year of collection), a company which buys and sells merchandise can still usually employ the cash method for other expenses.

A larger business which is less flexible and needs more formal financial statements will most likely use the accrual method. This hinders it in manipulating the timing of deductions and revenues. But it probably couldn't as easily take advantage of year-end tax planning as the smaller firm, anyway.

It is important to remember that exceptions exist for both the cash and accrual methods. If you own a cash method business, don't use all your cash to prepay rent, interest, and insurance. Although the deductions *might* be allowed by the IRS, your chances of deducting other types of prepaid expenses (such as advertising, expendable supplies, or property taxes) on your tax return would be much better.

Likewise, an accrual method business owner should be careful about accepting large payments for rent which cover periods far into the future. If he does not plan to raise the rent during that period, and really wants the cash, the 30 or 40 percent or more of the payment that he will lose as taxes this year may be worth it. But if regular payments with escalating rents could be averaged out over a number of years, tax planning and lower average annual income would bring him a smaller overall tax bill.

Whatever the method used by your business, your only hope for postponing taxes into later years is to look ahead to the end of the year, rather than only living day to day. If you have any flexibility to decide the year in which various revenues and expenses will appear on your tax return, some or all of your taxes can be pushed into later years.

If borrowing interest-free from the IRS reduces your need to borrow at ridiculous rates from the local banker, what better result can you ask of tax planning? Where else can a little forethought get you an interest rate of zero these days?

8

Inflation
Can Beat Taxes:
LIFO Inventory

When you go to the supermarket, do you reach to the back of the milk case to get the fresher milk? Do you take bread from the rear of the bread display? If so, you are aware that many grocery stores put their older merchandise to the front of the shelf to sell it quickly, then place the fresher items at the rear, since it will be longer before they're stale.

This is what tax law refers to as "first-in, first-out" inventory flow or FIFO. The older units are sold first; the newer ones, later.

On the other hand, some large manufacturing businesses buy coal or coke to feed their furnaces. They heap the fuel into a large mound and use the materials from the top or outside of the pile first. When new fuel is bought, it is thrown on top of the remaining heap and is used before any of the older materials. The material on the bottom of the pile may never be used.

This is called "last-in, first-out" flow or LIFO. The newer units are used first; the older ones later.

Actual Versus Assumed Flow of Units

We've been looking at actual flows of units—loaves of bread, cartons of milk, tons of coal and coke. We examined how they really enter and leave the business.

One odd thing about tax law is that it is not usually important whether you show the actual flow of goods on your tax return or say that their flow was different. A supermarket which has an actual first-in, first-out (FIFO) flow of merchandise can assume, for tax purposes, that last-in, first-out (LIFO) was used. A manufacturing business could say on its tax return that it used FIFO for its fuel, even if it did not.

Why should it matter which method is assumed for the tax return?

It is important because the method chosen will help determine the amount of what will be the largest deduction many merchandising and manufacturing companies have on their tax returns. This deduction, called "Cost of Goods Sold," will usually be larger, during a period of inflation, if you tell the IRS that you used LIFO (regardless of what method you actually used).

And the larger your Cost of Goods sold deduction, the smaller will be your taxable income *and* income taxes. Your business operations might be summarized on a tax return as follows:

	Sales	$ x,xxx
−	Cost of Goods Sold	xxx
=	Gross Profit	$ xxx
−	Operating Expenses	xx
=	Taxable Income	$ xx

Since your taxes are figured on Taxable Income, the smaller you can make it, the smaller will be your tax bill. Increasing your Cost of Goods Sold deduction is one way to do this.

What Are Inventory and Cost of Goods Sold?

"Inventory" or "merchandise" or "merchandise inventory" is anything you buy so that you can resell it at a profit. This could include anything from shoes to appliances to subdivided parcels of land.

The Cost of Goods Sold deduction represents the cost of inventory which you sold during the year. If 200 units were sold, the deduction is the cost assumed for those 200 units. The sales price of the units is revenue. If the units sold for $1 each, Sales for the year would be $200 (200 units x $1). If their cost was 50 cents each, the Cost of Goods Sold deduction would be $100 (200 units x $.50).

Two facts, however, complicate the situation and allow forward-looking people to pay less taxes than others do.

The first fact is that you may have sold 200 units during the year, but you no doubt had some inventory in stock at the beginning of the year and some left at the end of the year.

The other fact is that in a period of inflation, the prices of inventory that a company buys keep rising. The items we assumed were purchased for 50 cents probably actually cost 45 cents at the first of the year, but kept going up until they were costing 55 cents each at the end of the year. In addition, the units you had in stock at the beginning of the year probably only cost 40 cents, because they were purchased last year.

These two facts are present in almost every situation involving merchandise today. They enable your choice of inventory method to make what can be an enormous difference in your Cost of Goods Sold deduction and, consequently, in your income taxes for the year.

Inflation and LIFO Can Help You

The cost of what you buy to resell or use in manufacturing will probably be higher every time you purchase it during a period of inflation. For illustrative purposes, let's assume extreme price increases for your purchase of five units of the same product during a year. The cost of the first is $1; the second, $2; the third, $3; the fourth, $4; and the fifth, $5.

Assume, further, that you sell two units during the year. (Remember, it doesn't usually matter which two you show as sold on your tax return.)

FIFO would put the $1 and $2 units (earliest purchases) on your tax return as the units sold. Thus, Cost of Goods Sold would be the total of the two, or $3. LIFO tells the tax people that you sold the $5 and $4 units (latest purchases), making your Cost of Goods Sold a total of $9.

The actual flow of goods may have been the sale of the first *or* last two units purchased, but it is the flow *assumed* that counts. You are allowed to assume, by using LIFO, that the last units were sold first. This makes your Cost of Goods Sold deduction much larger than it would otherwise be.

Naturally this is both a simplified and extreme example, but we can say that LIFO will normally give a higher Cost of Goods Sold when the cost of the merchandise you buy keeps rising. This is precisely why many businesses have switched to LIFO from other methods. It almost always gives a larger deduction during a period of inflation. Consequently, taxes are lower and the cash available for reinvestment is higher.

Actually, LIFO only postpones taxes again and again as new purchases are made at higher prices, but the cash saved because of lower taxes can be used to buy more inventory, to acquire needed equipment, and for other purposes.

For example, a small hardware store whose only asset is merchandise might have the following differences:

	With LIFO	With FIFO
Beginning Inventory	$ 75,000	$ 75,000
Purchases	100,000	100,000
Merchandise Available for Sale	$175,000	$175,000
Ending Inventory	75,000	86,250
Cost of Goods Sold	$100,000	$ 88,750

Since LIFO assumes that the most recent purchases are sold first, the low-cost beginning inventory in our example remains unsold to become low-cost ending inventory ($75,000).

FIFO assumes that the earliest units are sold first. So, higher-cost merchandise purchased during the year becomes the ending inventory ($86,250), causing the Cost of Goods Sold to be $11,250 less than with LIFO.

An $11,250 difference in Cost of Goods Sold yields the same difference in taxable income. If the owner of this store is in the 40 percent tax bracket, his income taxes would be approximately $4,500 less this year by using LIFO (40% of $11,250).

Continued increases in the cost of the merchandise he buys and changes in his tax bracket could cause the tax savings to be even larger in succeeding years. But reinvesting only $4,500 per year at 16 percent interest compounded annually for about 15 years would increase his wealth by $250,000 by the end of that time. So, by doing nothing other than switching inventory methods, he can make his net worth a quarter of a million dollars higher than it would be if he used FIFO.

A Small Thorn

In exchange for using LIFO on your tax return, the IRS generally expects you to use the same method on the financial statements you show to bankers, prospective investors, and others. Just as LIFO produces a lower taxable income for your tax return, it will probably yield lower net income on the income statement. It will also result in a smaller inventory figure on the balance sheet when you say that your earliest (lowest-cost) purchases are the inventory remaining.

Many bankers have had a basic college accounting course. They realize the impact which different inventory methods have on your tax return and financial statements. These people should recognize your foresight and act accordingly.

But among naive lenders and investors, this can cause difficulties. They may insist on lending or investing less than they would if your inventory, taxable income, *and* taxes were higher.

Rather than pay higher taxes to impress potential lenders, you may want to just verbally explain the effect of LIFO, telling them what your inventory and earnings would otherwise be. If they still don't understand, remember that you keep more cash with LIFO. As a consequence, you will probably need to borrow less.

Important Points

If your business buys and sells inventory, you'll most likely have a stock of merchandise at the beginning and end of the year. You will purchase inventory during the year and take a tax deduction for what you sell. Since the Cost of Goods Sold can be such a large part of your annual deductions, even a small percentage increase in it because you use LIFO may result in a sizeable change in your tax bill.

This is one of the few places where inflation can be used to help cut your taxes. The money saved by lowering taxes can then help battle the effects of inflation on your enterprise. Reinvesting the cash should enable you to operate at a higher volume than someone else who insists on using FIFO (and paying a larger tax bill).

And by earning money on the cash saved, the process of compound interest can help build your business capital and personal wealth more quickly. Remember, just $4,500 per year of extra earnings from using LIFO could tack $250,000 or more onto your net worth in only 15 years.

PART THREE

Incorporating Could Make Your Life Better

9

A Corporation Might Lower Your Taxes

Regardless of the form in which your business is organized, you have a silent partner. His name is Uncle Sam. In return for certain unspecified services, you split your profits with him.

Uncle Sam knows, as does any other partner, that a business can grow only if part of its profits are reinvested. But Uncle Sam is a spender. He doesn't save or reinvest anything. He depends on you to do that.

To increase the amount which is reinvested annually in your business, you must increase your share of total profits. You can do this by working harder to raise the overall earnings of the business. Or you can increase your share by cutting Uncle Sam's portion.

Fortunately for you, people who own their own businesses have access to a large variety of tax breaks which can reduce the government's share of what they earn. The amount you can reinvest is easily raised by taking advantage of any of a number of generous tax-saving techniques.

Reinvesting the Most Income Possible

A business, like a savings account, increases in size with compound growth. While a savings account may grow at five or six percent compound interest, a successful business can be built up at a much faster rate. This difference is due to the fact that, in the U.S., risk is rewarded. Investing in a business presents greater risk than placing your cash in a savings account. So, a business can provide a greater return on your money.

What kind of growth should you expect?

If you invest $3,000 per year in a savings account and let each deposit grow at a five percent compound rate, you'll finish the twentieth year with almost $100,000.

Making the same 20 annual investments at a ten percent annual growth rate would yield a balance of about $170,000 at the end of that time.

At 20 percent, your total would be over half a million dollars at the end of 20 years.

Cutting your tax bill would increase the annual investment you could make. For example, doubling the $3,000 yearly investment in your business to $6,000 by saving taxes would allow you to accumulate (at a 20 percent growth rate) over $1 million by the end of 20 years.

Each of the tax breaks explained in this book is designed to do exactly that—to let you reinvest cash in your business which would otherwise be taken away as taxes. Tax breaks will help you to reach your financial goals. If you can reinvest just $17,000 each year for the next 30 years at a 20 percent growth rate, your business will be worth $20 million.

And one possible way to save the earnings you need in order to do exactly that is to incorporate your business, then take full advantage of the benefits tax law provides to corporations.

Your Sole Proprietorship

American business is conducted with three different types of organizations—sole proprietorships, partnerships, and corporations. You can see examples of each type wherever you look, from small shops to international conglomerates. Each form of business organization offers both advantages and disadvantages.

The sole proprietorship is a flexible, convenient form of organization which is easy to start and dissolve. To begin a sole proprietorship, you don't even need a bank account. You just start doing business.

The ten-year-old who makes pot holders or cookies and sells them door to door is the owner of a sole proprietorship. Similarly, a furniture store which has $500,000 of annual sales and has been in business for over 30 years may be a sole proprietorship.

Although this form of organization is informal and easy to start, it has certain legal disadvantages. The owner *is* the business. The business doesn't really exist apart from him. So, creditors or injured parties can sue the owner directly. If he becomes ill or incompetent or dies, the business may not survive.

The IRS also does not view a sole proprietorship as being separate from its owner. Business revenues and expenses must be shown on a page or pages attached to the owner's own personal income tax return. Any net profit is added to his other revenues. A loss is used to cut the owner's income from other sources.

This means that the income of a sole proprietorship is taxed at whatever rates the owner himself pays taxes. If he is in the 24 percent bracket, he'll pay 24 cents of each dollar to Uncle Sam. If he is in the 50 percent bracket, he must pay half.

How Partners Are Taxed

Like sole proprietorships, partnerships are flexible and convenient business organizations. But the partnership, which brings two or more people into business together, can often gather a larger amount of capital than can a sole proprietorship. By pooling their financial resources, several individuals may be able to conduct much more business than any one of them could handle alone.

Unfortunately, the partnership form of organization also has disadvantages. It could expose you to unforeseen risks.

Sometimes one or more partners appear to be acting for the partnership and can get all partners into a deal that most of them never wanted. You must choose your partners carefully.

Like a sole proprietor, a partner usually has unlimited liability. A creditor of the partnership can sue each partner individually. Also, in some states, if a partner dies, becomes disabled, or withdraws from the business, the partnership is automatically terminated. A new partnership must be formed.

Unless a comprehensive partnership agreement is drawn and annual audits by a CPA are conducted, disagreements among partners can destroy what would otherwise be a prosperous business.

Partnerships file their own tax returns separate from those of their owners. But the return filed for a partnership is mainly just for informational purposes. The income or loss of a partnership is divided and placed on the partners' individual tax returns. Like the profit of a sole proprietorship, the income of a partnership is taxed at each owner's personal tax rates. If that happens to be 50 percent, then half of a partner's share of profits is taken by the IRS.

The Subchapter S Corporation

The income or loss of a Subchapter S corporation (Sub S) is handled almost like that of a partnership. It is allocated to individual stockholders and placed on their own tax returns. This can be an enormous advantage if a business is currently operating at a loss, because each owner's share of the loss can be used to reduce his individual income taxes.

If a Sub S divides profits among its owners, they'll be taxed on them as if they were showing partnership profits on their tax returns. But a Sub S does have certain legal advantages which a partnership does not.

Sub S status is just between you and the IRS. As far as your state is concerned, a Sub S is just another corporation. So, the liability of Sub S owners to creditors and others is limited. If a partner becomes disabled or dies, a Sub S continues as if nothing happened. And part or all of the ownership of a Sub S can be transferred to someone else easily by giving or selling shares of stock.

Unfortunately, the circumstances in which a Sub S can be employed are more limited than for other types of corporations. Chapter 12 explains when a Sub S can help you and how best to use this form of organization to cut your tax bill.

Using a Regular Corporation to Save Taxes

The corporate form of business has advantages. It may enable you to raise larger amounts of capital than would be possible with a sole proprietorship or partnership. (Almost all large businesses are corporations or groups of corporations.) Your ownership interest can be partly or completely sold or given to another person just by transferring shares of stock to him. And your liability is limited. People sue the corporation, not you. Your personal assets are relatively safe.

Like other forms of business organization, the corporation also has its drawbacks. It can be costly to form if you hire an attorney. Permission is required from your state to form the corporation and may be needed to make later changes such as increasing the number of shares of stock it is authorized to issue. Board of director meetings and required paperwork cut down on the flexibility of the corporation.

But, in the right circumstances, a corporation can save you bundles of income taxes.

Lower Tax Rates Could Result

A regular corporation files its own tax return and pays its own taxes. No earnings are taxed to stockholders unless part of the profits are paid out to them as salaries, dividends, or other distributions.

Most people are surpised to learn that while they're paying taxes through the nose, a corporation's tax rates are relatively lenient:

Naturally, tax rates for both individuals and corporations are subject to change. But you can see that there's a fair-sized discrepancy between what you might pay Uncle Sam on your individual tax return and what a corporation would. As you approach the 40 or 50 percent tax bracket, a corporation earning the same amount may still be in the 18 percent tax bracket.

A Corporation's Taxable Income	A Corporation's Tax Rates
$ -0- to $ 25,000	15%
$25,000 to $ 50,000	18%
$50,000 to $ 75,000	30%
$75,000 to $ 100,000	40%
Over $100,000	46%

For example, on personal income of $50,000, you might pay more than $14,000 in income taxes, while a corporation would pay only $9,000—a difference of more than $5,000.

This fact may irritate you until you understand that anyone is welcome to form a corporation and take advantage of these favorable rates. If you already have your own business, you can incorporate it. If not, you can form a corporation and start or buy a business.

A corporation may be the perfect form of organization to own your business, especially if you presently receive or anticipate large income from sources in addition to your business. By dividing your total income between the corporate tax return and your own personal return, your total tax bill may be lower than if you placed all the income on your personal return.

Let's say that you have total earnings from investments and a business of $150,000. By placing all this on your own tax return (married, filing jointly), you'd pay around $60,000 in taxes.

Assume, instead, that you incorporate your business so that $75,000 is taxed to your corporation. The remaining $75,000 goes directly to your individual return. This combination would probably drop your annual tax liability to around $40,000—a savings of $20,000 each year. (You recall that investing only $17,000 annually at 20 percent compound interest produces $20 million in 30 years.)

Solving the Dividend Problem

Although a corporation may pay less tax on a specific amount of income than you would, some of that income *could* end up being taxed twice. This can happen when money which has already been taxed to the corporation is paid out to its owners as dividends. Dividends can't be deducted by the corporation, but they are taxed to the stockholders.

One way to get around this problem is to drain cash you need out of the corporation as salaries, rent, interest, and royalties for effort and property you provide to the business. Such payments are taxable to you, but they can be deducted by the corporation. So, they're taxed only once.

Earnings you do not need can then be left in the corporation. The double-taxation problem crops up mainly when profits are paid out of the business to stockholders.

Of course, traps set in the tax law can cause difficulties when you pay yourself too much salary or retain earnings in the business for no apparent reason. Chapter 22 explains where these traps lie and how to avoid them.

Fringe Benefits

Each of us has seen corporations provide enviable fringe benefits (company cars, retirement plans, and numerous others) to stockholders.

Everybody seems to want fringe benefits. But exactly how can they help you save taxes?

Fringe benefits save taxes because many of them can be deducted by your corporation, but *not* taxed to you. So, they are earnings which are never taxed at all.

Contrast this with:

1) Dividends—taxed once to your corporation as profits, then again to you when you receive them; and

2) Salary, rent, interest, and royalties—deducted by your corporation but taxed to you.

A sole proprietorship or partnership can offer its owner or owners company cars, limited retirement plans (Chapter 4), and a few other niceties. But neither can hope to compete with the list of tax-free benefits which you can have through your own corporation.

Fringe benefits are discussed in greater detail in Chapter 11.

Dividends Your Corporation Receives

Although you are taxed on all the dividends you receive from your own corporation or from investments in shares of stock, a corporation might not be. Only 15 percent of the qualifying dividends a corporation receives from most other domestic corporations are taxed to it.

This means that while you are taxed on $1 of dividends, your corporation would place only 15 cents of the same dollar on its own tax return. By the time you talk about applying a lower corporate tax rate to only 15 percent of what you'd show on your personal tax return, letting your corporation own part or all of your investments begins to look like a pretty good idea.

For example, assume that you receive $20,000 of dividends from investments in stock during the year. If you are in the 40 percent tax bracket, Uncle Sam takes about $8,000 (40 percent of $20,000).

But let's say that your corporation owns your investments for you. First of all, only 15 percent of the $20,000, or $3,000, would be taxed. Then, if it is in the 18 percent bracket, your corporation would owe $540 in taxes. This is $7,460 less than you would owe.

While allowing your corporation to own investments and pay less tax than you'd owe is perfectly legal, your corporation will need to also generate income from business operations. If too much of its revenue is from "passive" sources such as dividends or interest, the personal holding company tax (Chapter 22) could apply.

Other Possible Tax Advantages

A corporation may be able to offer you other, less tangible advantages in your effort to save taxes.

For example, if your business has been unprofitable for several years, the IRS *could* move to limit the deductions you've taken in those years. But some authorities believe that this is less likely to happen if your business is incorporated. The fact that you have gone to the trouble of forming a corporation adds weight to the idea that you are serious about your business and that expenses your company has are truly business (not personal) expenses.

Other tax experts even believe that your chances of facing a tax audit may be less if part of your income is earned by your corporation, especially if your individual income tax return would otherwise show high income.

Think Ahead to Selling Your Business

At the moment, building a successful business is probably foremost in your mind. After you've built it, however, you may want to move on to other things—such as a beach in the Bahamas.

Although people often see a business as an ideal route to financial independence and, perhaps, early retirement, they don't think about what will happen (tax-wise) when they sell it.

Most folks assume that their gain from selling a business will be a leniently-taxed long-term capital gain. But, if your business is a sole proprietorship, selling it could cause a tax disaster. The sale of a sole proprietorship is the same as the sale of its individual assets. If most of what your business owns are items such as inventory, accounts receivable, and depreciated equipment and buildings, part or all of your gain from selling the business will be unprotected ordinary income. And this type of income is taxed as severely as salary, interest, or commissions.

Even when you sell your interest in a partnership, part of the resulting gain could be ordinary income.

But shares of stock in a corporation are a capital asset. When you've owned them for more than a year, selling them at a gain will result in a long-term capital gain (Chapter 19).

For example, let's say that you are in the 50 percent tax bracket. Taxes would take only about 20 percent of a long-term capital gain. So, if you sell shares of stock in your business at a $100,000 gain, your taxes would amount to about $20,000 (20 percent of $100,000).

On the other hand, selling a sole proprietorship for a gain of $100,000 could result in a much larger tax bill. If the gain is entirely ordinary income, your taxes on the sale would amount to $50,000 (your 50 percent tax bracket multiplied by the $100,000 gain). Your tax liability would be $30,000 more than if you were selling shares of stock.

You may also find that a convenient way to sell part of your business while retaining an interest in it is to sell shares of stock in your corporation. (You merely sell part of your stock, rather than all of it.)

If you prefer not to incorporate your business right away, you may want to consider doing so a few years before you sell it. You'll be able to transfer your business assets to a corporation without taxable gain (Chapter 10). Then, you can later sell your corporation at a capital gain.

Important Points

Each of the three major forms of business organization has both advantages and disadvantages. Depending upon the size and type of business you have, legal or tax considerations may completely rule out one or two of these forms.

You may even find it useful, across your business career, to start with one type of organization and eventually switch to another.

Although the sole proprietorship is easy to start, you may eventually see legal or tax disadvantages. You're extremely vulnerable to legal problems. And business income is taxed on your personal tax return at your own high tax rates.

Similarly, the partnership form of organization can involve you in legal difficulties. And income is funneled out of the business to be taxed on partners' own tax returns.

A Subchapter S corporation provides protection from legal problems as a regular corporation might, but passes income or loss out to owners' tax returns as if it were a partnership. When a business expects several years of losses, the Sub S form of organization can save considerable taxes for its shareholders. They can use losses immediately to offset income they earn elsewhere.

Although it is less flexible than a sole proprietorship or a partnership, a regular corporation may provide possible advantages. Since corporate tax rates are often lower than individual tax rates, splitting your income with your own corporation can yield lower taxes. Tax-free fringe benefits add icing to the cake. And special deals such as the way in which corporations are taxed on most dividends add further to the reasons for owning a corporation.

When the time comes to sell your business, you may find it worthwhile to sell stock you own rather than the individual assets of a sole proprietorship. If you're selling a valuable business, the difference in your tax bill between disposing of a corporation and a sole proprietorship can be large.

Your decision about which form of organization your business should be isn't one to make lightly. When you think about 1) your net profits across the next 20 or 30 years and 2) your gain on the eventual sale of the business itself, even a small tax advantage could add up to some big savings.

Whatever business form you choose, give at least some thought to the tax-saving opportunities which your own corporation could provide.

10

Selling Assets
to Your Corporation
Tax-Free

As you saw in Chapter 9, doing business as a corporation can have both legal and tax advantages. This may lead you to start your next enterprise as a corporation or to incorporate a going business.

Your corporation can buy the assets it needs from two sources—1) you or 2) other people and businesses.

Normally, when you sell something, you're taxed on any gain. This chapter shows how your new or older corporation can buy assets from you without your owing a tax bill on the deal.

For example, let's assume that you own a self-service laundry as a sole proprietorship or partnership. If you sell washers, dryers, a building, or other assets to outsiders, you are taxed on any gain.

Let us say, instead, that you decide to incorporate the business. When you do so, you are selling your washers, dryers, building, and other assets to your new corporation. Tax rules offer you a way to avoid taxes on any gain on this sale.

Similarly, if you sell assets to a corporation you've owned for some time (rather than just started), the same tax-saving idea applies.

The IRS asks only that you put your asset or assets into the business in exchange for stock or other securities in the corporation and that you own at least 80 percent of all classes of stock immediately after the deal.

Meeting the 80 Percent Test

Tax law wants to let you off the hook only if the property you put into the corporation has basically the same ownership and control afterward that it had when it belonged to you.

Assume, for instance, that you sell your laundry equipment to a nationwide corporation. In exchange, the corporation issues you stock until you own ten percent of the enterprise. With only ten percent ownership, you would be hard-pressed to exercise the same control over the equipiment that you previously had. You can't paint it green with orange stripes. You cannot decide which repairman to call for help. So the deal is taxable as if you'd sold for cash.

But, what if you put your property into a corporation for stock and own 80 to 100 percent of all the business' stock right after the sale? In this case, you would still have about the same control as before. Technically your property would now be owned by the corporation. But you could still tell the corporation what to do. So, you'd still control the property. The sale of your assets probably would not be taxable.

A New Corporation You Form

As you have seen, this tax-saving method can be used if you form a corporation to take over a business or other assets that you've owned for some time. You do not need to own all the stock in the new business. But, if you are the only person putting property into the new corporation, you'd better wind up with at least 80 percent ownership.

Assume that you have owned a hardware store for several years. The legal and tax advantages of the corporate form of business persuade you to incorporate your store. You receive nothing but stock for your hardware business and wind up with 80 to 100 percent of the total stock in the new corporation. You're not taxed for selling your business.

An Existing Corporation You Own

Let's say that your corporation runs the hardware store for a few years. Finally you decide that the business needs a car. You put your personal car into the corporation. The corporation issues stock to you. As long as you own 80 to 100 percent of the corporation's stock after the deal, you are still okay.

But what if you've sold stock during those intervening years until you now own only 79 percent after putting your car into the enterprise? In this case, you are taxed on the sale as if you'd sold the vehicle to a stranger for cash.

Why?

You failed the 80 percent test.

An Existing Corporation You Don't Own

It does not matter whether you own zero percent or 100 percent of an existing corporation *before* a deal as long as you own 80 to 100 percent *afterward*.

Assume that your brother has a corporation which owns land. You transfer cattle you own into the business. The corporation issues you stock and, as a result, you wind up with 85 percent ownership in the enterprise. Since you got at least 80 percent of the stock, you probably don't owe any taxes on the deal.

If you had put your cattle into the corporation for 79 percent ownership, or anything less, you'd be taxed.

A Sale By Several Persons

You do not have to go through such a deal alone in order to avoid taxes. If two or more people transfer property to a corporation for stock and, right after the exchange, they have 80 to 100 percent ownership *together,* they meet the 80 percent test.

Making It Tax-Free

Let's say that three people want to pool various pieces of real estate to give themselves a larger operating base. They can put their properties into a corporation which already exists. Or they can start a new one. But they have all got to put their assets into the business simultaneously, and together they must own at least 80 percent of the corporation's stock after the transfer, for the transfer to be tax free.

Frank has a $100,000 apartment building, George has a $200,000 office building, and Al has a $75,000 warehouse. They decide to incorporate. After the three simultaneously transfer their properties to the new corporation, none of them individually owns 80 percent. But together they own all of the stock (100 percent), which is more than enough to show that they still own and control the assets.

A "Single Transaction"

The transfers must be made in a single transaction. If Frank already owns a corporation which holds his apartments, and George and Al give their real estate to the business for stock, George and Al would wind up with only about 73 percent of the stock. This is because Frank already has $100,000 of the stock (assuming $1 par per share) by the time the other two receive $200,000 and $75,000 worth of stock for their assets. Frank doesn't transfer anything, but he still owns about 27 percent of the stock after the deal. So, George and Al only get about 73 percent of the stock in the trade.

Since George and Al own less than 80 percent of the corporation's stock, their transfer to the corporation is taxable as if they'd sold their properties to a stranger for cash. The fact that they own 100 percent of the stock *with* Frank is irrelevant. Only George and Al were involved in the transfer, and they now own less than 80 percent of the stock.

Let's assume, on the other hand, that Frank has 100,000 shares of stock and that George and Al receive 400,000 shares for an office building, warehouse, and shopping center. The total number of shares is now 500,000 (Frank's 100,000 plus George and Al's 400,000). Even though Frank owned all of the corporation before, George and Al own 80 percent of the stock after their transfer. So, George and Al are not taxed on the sale.

Important Points

Advantages of the corporate form of doing business may, sooner or later, cause you to put assets into a corporation for stock. The corporation may be new or older, one you own, or one you don't own. You may be the only person transferring property into the business. Or you may be one of several.

Almost any asset could be traded to a corporation for stock—anything from inventory to equipment to a vacant lot. But you can't trade your *services* to the business for stock. Such an exchange would be taxable. Only assets can be put into the corporation.

Similarly, if the corporation gives you anything other than stock or other securities for your property, you may pay some taxes. Or, if the corporation assumes your mortgage on an asset and the mortgage is larger than your basis in the asset, you could wind up with a tax bill.

When you trade assets to a new or existing corporation for stock, tax law wants to be satisfied that control of the assets hasn't really changed because of the transfer. So, you and any other people putting in assets at the same time must have 80 to 100 percent ownership right after the exchange.

Although direct ownership of the items has technically changed, you have virtually complete control over the actual owner (your corporation). You can exercise about the same influence over the assets that you had before the transfer.

If you do not end up with at least 80 percent ownership, the IRS figures that you have given up control. You are taxed as if you had sold the property.

Selling assets to your own corporation tax-free could be one of the largest tax breaks you will ever use. It may not cut the taxes on your annual income. But it can help you avoid a huge tax bill on the sale of your assets to a corporation.

11

Deductible Fringe Benefits from Your Corporation

As you saw in Chapter 9, there are three ways to squeeze benefits out of your corporation:

1) You can pay yourself dividends, which have already been taxed once as earnings to your corporation and will now be taxed again as you receive them.

2) You can pay yourself salary, interest, rent, or royalties for the use of your labor or property. These amounts are taxed only once—to you. The corporation deducts them.

3) Certain fringe benefits your corporation provides to you are deductible by your business, but not taxable to you. So, nobody pays taxes on them.

The third type of corporate benefit, of course, is the best. It's one of the few ways you can help yourself in a completely tax-free manner. And it is a big reason why you should strongly consider the corporate form of organization for your business.

Consider what happens when you pay for an item you need with your salary. First the salary is taxed. Only the remainder can be used as you choose. For example, if you are in the 33 percent tax bracket, each $1.50 of earnings leaves you only $1.00 to spend as you wish (taxes take $.50).

Because it is deductible, your corporation may be able to give you the same item by spending only $1.00 (not $1.50). It spends the money *before* taxes, then deducts the expenditure.

When you move into a higher tax bracket, the contrast between what something costs you and what your corporation must pay for it can be even more dramatic.

Company Car and Plane

The IRS realizes that a certain amount of business travel inside your city or town and to other locations is necessary. You can move from place to place by public transportation. Or you can use your own car or airplane.

Owning a car or plane can have big tax advantages. You'll generate a sizeable tax credit to cut your taxes dollar for dollar just by purchasing one (Chapter 16). Then, excellent depreciation deductions provide tax shelter for your income across the car or plane's life (Chapter 15). Your tax savings in the first year or so of ownership may be more than the down payment on the item.

For example, assume that your corporation buys a $12,000 company car for a $1,500 down payment in December of this year. Even though the first payment isn't due until January or February, the corporation immediately receives a $720 tax credit and a $2,910 depreciation deduction.

If it is in the 40 percent tax bracket, the $1,500 down payment saves your corporation almost $1,900 in taxes for this year. Next year, your business can deduct interest, more depreciation, gasoline, taxes, insurance, and other costs.

And you'll have the advantage of using tax-free a vehicle you don't even personally own.

Basically the same tax-saving opportunities are available with your own corporate plane, whether it seats 3 or 300. If your business requires a great deal of travel, a small corporate plane can help you reach commercial or non-commercial airports on any schedule you like. A large number of businessmen have recognized this fact and now pilot their own aircraft.

In certain circumstances, it may be better for you to personally own the car or plane and lease it to your corporation. While you're in the 40 percent tax bracket, for instance, your corporation may only be in the 18 percent bracket (Chapter 9). This means that the investment credit, depreciation deductions, and other tax breaks would benefit your tax return more than they would your corporation's return. You might save $2,000 of taxes in the year of purchase while your corporation would save less than $1,000 as a result of its naturally lower tax bracket.

So, you could personally buy the item and take all of the tax benefits on your individual tax return. These would offset the rent your corporation paid you for its use. And the result would be a tax-free fringe benefit with higher than expected deductions.

Corporate cars and planes are often used for personal purposes. But you should know that if the IRS suspects this of you, they will call your personal use "taxable compensation." Each mile you drive a corporate car or fly a corporate plane for personal enjoyment, rather than business purposes, is technically taxable like salary.

Qualified Stock Options

Rather than paying yourself additional salary, you may wish to give yourself options to buy stock in your corporation at attractive prices. This fringe benefit is especially important when a corporation is owned by several stockholders.

There are two types of stock options—those which are "nonqualified" and those which are "qualified" or "incentive" stock options. "Nonqualified" stock options are usually taxed when you receive them. "Incentive" stock options aren't.

In order to take advantage of incentive stock options, you must:

1) Keep the stock for more than a year after you exercise the option;

2) Keep the stock for more than two years after the date the option is granted;

3) Work continuously for the corporation granting the option until three months before you exercise it;

4) Be certain that the options are granted and exercised according to a written incentive stock option plan which meets several other requirements.

Giving yourself stock options Uncle Sam's way means that you are not taxed until you sell the stock. At that time, you'll have a long-term, leniently-taxed capital gain.

If you decide at some point that you want to sell your business, take a careful look at the condition of your stock options. The sales agreement should be written to allow you to meet all the requirements for special treatment of your options.

For example, you may need to continue working for the corporation until requirement 3) is fulfilled *and* until you've met the holding rules of 1) and 2).

While stock options can be an excellent way to compensate yourself in some circumstances (you may be able to give yourself options to buy up to $100,000 of stock each year), they can be tricky. Have your tax advisor accompany you every step of the way.

Tax-Free Housing and Meals

Your corporation may be able to provide to you tax-free meals and housing which it can deduct. Instead of paying taxes on your salary and then buying meals or housing, this is another case where the earnings that buy the benefits would never be taxed.

In order to do this, the corporation would, first of all, need to pay for the meals or housing directly. The IRS does not like to see your corporation reimburse you for these items.

To provide you with tax-free meals, the corporation will also have to require you to eat on its premises. Of course, this may not be as difficult as it sounds. Small business owners are often needed at their places of business during meal times. And executive dining rooms are common.

Similarly, if you are going to receive tax-free housing, the corporation would need a good reason requiring you to live on its premises. But since numerous corporate officers receive this benefit, the possibilities look good.

When your corporation owns the house in which you live, it may be able to squeeze excellent tax shelter from depreciation (Chapter 13) and other items such as insurance and utilities which otherwise might not be deductible.

One technicality to watch out for is that any tax-free housing provided should normally be *on* the business premises. It's difficult for your corporation to justify requiring you to live in corporate-owned housing across town.

The IRS' main fear about this potentially valuable benefit is that your corporation will not have a valid reason for providing tax-free meals and/or housing to you. So, in order to enjoy this tax break, you'll need to lay your ground-work in advance for satisfying the government's curiosity—perhaps even to the extent of recording the reasons in your corporate minutes.

Health and Accident Insurance

One of the most basic tax-free benefits your corporation can provide is often overlooked by people who incorporate their businesses. This is the payment of premiums on health and accident insurance (deductible by the corporation, but not taxed to you).

The attractiveness of this benefit is enhanced by the fact that medical reimbursements you receive on the insurance bought are also normally tax-free to you. Only when insurance proceeds you receive take the form of wage continuation payments are you likely to be taxed. Even then, you won't pay taxes in every case.

Group Term Life Insurance

Similarly, your corporation can pay and deduct the premiums on a group term life insurance policy for you up to a policy face of

$50,000. This benefit is not taxed to you. Neither would the proceeds of the policy be taxed to your beneficiaries upon your death. So, you get a double benefit.

Note that the insurance must be "term" life—pure insurance protection without a savings feature. And it must be a group policy.

The benefits of this tax break aren't as great as those provided by others. This, combined with the requirement that the insurance be issued under a "group" policy may cause you to wait until your corporation has several employees before you take advantage of tax-free insurance premiums.

Tax-Free Death Benefits

While you're having fringe benefit plans drawn up, you may as well consider one more. Up to $5,000 of tax-free cash can be provided to your beneficiaries in the event of your death.

Admittedly, you can only take advantage of this tax break the hard way. But with the tax problems and other bills they could face upon your death, your family might truly appreciate $5,000 of tax-free income.

As with many of the other benefits explained in this chapter, your corporation can deduct the payment—even though it's not taxed to your beneficiaries.

Travel and Entertainment

Chapter 1 explains in some detail how to get your largest deductions for business entertainment and out-of-town meals and lodging. The reason the subject is also included in a chapter on corporate fringe benefits is to remind you that living well can be a natural result of conducting your business.

As long as your expenditures for entertainment and out-of-town meals and lodging are reasonable in amount and meet a few other requirements (Chapter 1), the IRS cannot tell you how to live. If you want to stay at the Hilton and eat steak or if you choose to entertain clients in appropriate style, Uncle Sam probably won't argue.

Some people might suggest that funds used for business travel and entertainment are not reinvested in the corporation, so they're wasted. But, in a sense, they *are* reinvested. If they are used sensibly to increase your list of customers or clients and to open up new areas of business, amounts spent on travel and entertainment actually do build up your business. And, if you enjoy entertaining and traveling, you're doubly benefited.

Pension and Profit-Sharing Plans

Although Keogh plans and IRA's (Chapter 4) permit owners of unincorporated businesses to accumulate considerable amounts for retirement, corporate plans can be better.

The basic idea behind retirement plans for owners of both unincorporated and incorporated businesses is the same—contributions made to a plan are deducted by the business but not taxed to anyone until cash is later paid out. Earnings on funds accumulated in such plans are also tax exempt.

The annual limit on what you can invest/deduct with an IRA is $2,000; with a Keogh plan, $15,000 ($30,000 in 1984 and later). Corporate defined contribution plans have a $30,000 yearly limit on what can be invested and deducted for your benefit. The maximum for a corporate profit-sharing plan is 25 percent of your compensation.

Vesting for employees need not be immediate in corporate plans. This means that employees who quit their jobs with your corporation may not be able to take with them the contributions you have made on their behalf. Amounts forfeited may be divided among those persons (including you) who remain in the plan.

As with Keogh plans, a business owner who has employees may find that the contributions he must make for them can outweigh the advantages provided to himself by a tax-free pension or profit-sharing plan. A simple IRA for the owner of a corporation may provide satisfactory retirement security at far less cost.

But if you are running your corporation by yourself or with a few employees whom you want to benefit, by all means take a close look at corporate pension and profit-sharing plans. The size of annual investment/deductions and potential tax-free buildup of your fund can be astonishing.

Watch Your Cost/Benefit Ratio

Corporate pension and profit-sharing plans are not the only fringe benefits which must be shared with your employees in order for the benefits to be tax-free to you. So, the more employees you have, the more expensive certain fringe benefits can become.

When you have no employees or your employees are family members, you may be willing to put almost any amount of earnings into such benefits.

Otherwise, consider carefully the actual benefit you are going to personally receive and what it will cost you to take advantage of it. You may not wish to use all the benefits to which you're entitled.

Stay Away From "Hidden" Dividends

Dividends you receive from your business are earnings which wind up being taxed twice—once to your corporation and again when you receive them. Some types of dividends are obvious, such as when you write yourself a check and call it a "dividend." Others are not so obvious, but can still be construed as dividends and taxed twice.

For example, when you pay yourself more than what the IRS believes your salary should be, the excess becomes a "dividend" and is taxed twice instead of only once as your salary would be. If you pay yourself $100,000 during a year and the IRS successfully argues that only $60,000 should be salary, you'll still be taxed on the entire $100,000. But only $60,000 of it can be deducted by your corporation. The other $40,000 will be classed as a dividend (taxable to you, but not deductible by your corporation).

Similarly, using any fringe benefit in a way to which you are not entitled could have about the same result. If you use your company car for personal purposes, the value of that nonbusiness use is taxable to you.

Chapter 22 explains the most common tax traps (including "hidden" dividends) and shows the best ways to stay away from each.

Important Points

Letting your corporation pay for deductible fringe benefits is an excellent method of squeezing additional profits out of your business. The benefits are bought with dollars which are never subjected to taxes. Although they are deducted by your corporation, these expenditures are never taxed to you.

One of the first items you may wish to consider is a corporate car. Most businesses must have at least one auto in order to make sales, visit clients, or deliver products. And the tax savings in the first year or so of ownership can often outweigh the down payment required to buy the car.

Tax-free housing and/or meals is another benefit you may wish to examine. If your business needs you to stay on the premises, you may be able to save a great deal of money by paying for these necessities with before-tax dollars.

Travel and entertainment can be a pleasant way to build your business. The fact that entertainment and out-of-town meals and lodging are tax deductible can enable you to live in a better manner than you otherwise might.

Health and accident insurance may be another item which you'll like your corporation to pay. You are probably unable, on your own personal tax return, to deduct as large an amount of insurance premiums as your corporation can. Similarly, tax-free death benefits and group term life insurance are attractive benefits your corporation can provide.

As your business increases in size, stock options, pension plans, and profit-sharing plans can help you postpone the time at which your income is taxed. These are all methods for deferring parts of your earnings so that they are taxed in later years (when your total income and tax rates are lower).

It is important that any plan to pay your insurance or to defer your compensation be set up to follow all appropriate tax rules. A mistake could cost your corporation its deduction or might cause you to be taxed on your benefit.

Be selective in choosing the fringe benefits you ask your corporation to give you. Remember to evaluate the well-being each provides in light of its cost. And check for the possibility of "hidden" dividends.

If a benefit looks good after passing these tests, don't hesitate to use it. Although many small corporation owners might not think of giving themselves tax-free meals, or a company plane, or accident and health insurance, each of these deserves to be considered.

Deductible fringe benefits can be an important part of your overall tax-saving strategy. This is one of the few ways to buy yourself goods and services you want with profits which are not taxed to either your business or yourself.

12

Tax Advantages of a Subchapter S Corporation

Chapter 9 explained how doing business as a corporation may help you cut your overall tax bill, mainly by subjecting your business income to lower average tax rates. Deductible fringe benefits (Chapter 11) help to achieve the same purpose.

But corporations sometimes go through years when they have losses instead of earnings. This can especially be the case for the first few years after a business starts. It usually advertises heavily and tries to build up its list of customers. A corporation's losses may just accumulate until it has some income to use them against.

On the other hand, businesses which are organized as sole proprietorships or partnerships pass losses on to their owners. These losses are used immediately to save the owners taxes on their own personal tax returns by reducing income they earn elsewhere.

So, there doesn't seem to be a good way out, does there? If you want the advantages of a corporation—limited liability, easy transferability of ownership, continuity of life—you may not be able to use business losses to cut taxes this year. If you want to use losses to save taxes now, you can't have the legal advantages of a corporation.

This is where the Subchapter S (Sub S) corporation comes in handy. It gives you the best of both worlds.

How a Sub S Corporation Is Different

A regular corporation files its own tax return and pays its own taxes. Capital gains sometimes get special treatment (Chapter 20), but other income is taxed at normal corporate rates. Losses can only be used against the corporation's own profits—even if profits don't appear for several years.

A Sub S corporation funnels out its income and losses to its owners almost like a partnership might. So any income is taxed on the shareholders' own tax returns and any losses are used to cut their other income.

This is the case even though, as far as your own state is concerned, your business is just a corporation like any other. The tax status of the enterprise is strictly between you and the IRS. So, you get all the legal advantages of a corporation with the tax advantages of a partnership.

Dividing Up Regular Income and Losses

Sub S profits, losses, deductions, and credits are divided among shareholders by looking at their percentages of stock ownership on a daily basis. If you own 60 percent or 100 percent of the corporation's stock all year, you get 60 percent or 100 percent of any tax item for the year. But let us say that you begin the year with 60 percent ownership and move up to 80 percent ownership on July 1. Your average owner-ship for the year would be 70 percent, so this is the portion of any item you'd be able to take to your personal tax return.

Watch Out for These Traps

If you have or will have a Sub S corporation, you need to be careful about three things:

1) If it has a large amount of long-term capital gain in any single year, your Sub S *could* be taxed on part of the gain before the gain is

funneled out to the owners' tax returns. Fortunately, if your corporation is less than four years old or has been a Sub S for over three years, you probably will not be subject to this extra tax. Also, you usually won't run into this problem anyway, because the capital gains have to be more than half of the enterprise's taxable income for the year *and* must be over $25,000. But this is another place where you may need to carefully plan your sales of capital assets—possibly even using the installment sales method (Chapter 21) if you sell a large capital asset.

2) While you can request Sub S status either for a new corporation or for one which has been operating for several years, the new corporation has an advantage in one circumstance. A special income tax is applied when a corporation which has been a regular (non-Sub S) corporation is turned into a Sub S and subsequently earns more than 25 percent of its annual revenues as passive income such as rent or interest. This does not happen to a corporation you form with Sub S status in mind.

Since passive income can result from as simple an action as investing unneeded funds temporarily in savings accounts or marketable securities, a new corporation should be employed where possible. If you turn an existing corporation into a Sub S, keep an eye on the amount of passive (as opposed to operating) revenues you receive.

3) When you convert a non-Sub S corporation into a Sub S, you must also pay close attention to the amount of cash and property your enterprise distributes to you. While it can pay out with no tax effect accumulated earnings for years during which it has Sub S status, distribution of non-Sub S earnings will result in tax.

Let's say you converted to Sub S last year and earned $50,000 for the year. The first $50,000 you pay out to yourself will probably be tax-free. (You've already been taxed on it.) Depending on several factors, however, additional distributions could be taxed as dividends.

Qualifying as a Sub S

If it's going to let you have the best points of both a corporation and a partnership, the law figures that it can make you meet a few requirements. You must meet them before your business can become a Sub S. And, if you stop meeting them, you lose your Sub S status. Your corporation is then taxed as a regular (non-Sub S) corporation.

Number of Shareholders

A Sub S corporation can't have more than 35 shareholders. A husband and wife are normally counted as one shareholder for this purpose.

If you own all the stock of your corporation, you are not in any danger of losing your Sub S status because of this requirement. But let's say that you are one of 35 shareholders. Suddenly a husband and wife (treated as *one* of the 35) divorce, splitting their stock. Now there are 36 shareholders. The Sub S becomes a regular corporation and is taxed as such.

Or, what if there are already 35 shareholders and one sells part of his stock to someone else? Now there are 36 shareholders. The corporation loses its Sub S tax status.

Type of Shareholders

Since it is opposed to permitting more than 35 shareholders, tax law doesn't want you to get around this requirement by letting a parnership, corporation, or certain trusts be shareholders. If a partnership with 50 partners or a corporation with 75 owners became a shareholder in a Sub S, the 35-shareholder limit would be circumvented. That would never do.

So, a shareholder of a Sub S corporation can only be an individual, estate, or certain other type of trust. Any other kind of owner will prevent a corporation from becoming a Sub S or will terminate its Sub S status.

Type of Stock

A Sub S can usually have more than one class of stock authorized and *un*issued. But it can only have one class of stock issued and outstanding.

Type of Corporation

To become a Sub S, your corporation must be a domestic (U.S.) corporation. With few exceptions, a Sub S cannot be a member of an affiliated group of corporations (such as a parent-subsidiary arrangement).

How to Make Your Election

To have your corporation become a Sub S, you must get all shareholders to sign IRS Form 2553. If stock is owned by a married couple, normally both must sign.

If you are just starting a corporation and want it to be a Sub S from the beginning, you need to file the form with the IRS on or before the fifteenth day of the third month in the corporation's taxable year. So, if your corporation's year runs from January 1 through December 31, you must apply for Sub S status on or before March 15.

Missing the deadline means that the business will be taxed as a regular corporation this year but can become a Sub S next year.

When you already own a corporation which you want to turn into a Sub S (maybe you're expecting some losses and want them to pass through to your personal tax return), you can normally file the form during the tax year before you want it to become a Sub S. Your final deadline is the fifteenth day of the third month of the corporation's taxable year in which you wish to begin Sub S status.

Be sure to either hand carry the form to the appropriate IRS office or send it by registered mail. One day's delay by a careless clerk could cost you thousands of dollars in taxes.

Giving Up Your Sub S Status

Your Sub S corporation can go back to being taxed as a regular corporation in any number of ways—either because you want it to or because the IRS wants it to.

You Might Prefer Regular Corporate Tax

Sub S tax status is most useful when your business is going through one or more loss years. Losses are sent to your personal tax return, rather than held useless in the corporation.

But when your enterprise starts making money, the same tax-saving advantages explained in Chapter 9 apply. You may be able to cut your overall tax bill by allowing part of the income to be taxed to your corporation. This means giving up Sub S tax status and moving the business to regular corporate tax status.

How do you do it?

One way of changing to regular corporate taxes is for shareholders owning a majority of the corporation's stock to sign and file a consent form with the IRS. They must take this action no later than the fifteenth day of the third month of the corporation's taxable year.

For example, let's say that you want to change for the year 19B. Assume, further, that your corporation works on a calendar tax year (ending December 31). You'll have to file the consent form on or before March 15,19B for the change to be effective in 19B.

How The Change Could Happen, Anyway

You saw the rules a corporation has to meet *before* it can become a Sub S. Failing to live by those *after* the business becomes a Sub S may cause it to lose its favorable tax status. If it does, you often can't apply for Sub S status again for another five years.

So, if you find yourself with 36 shareholders, or a shareholder who is a partnership or corporation, or with two classes of stock outstanding, you could lose your tax status.

If your Sub S status is terminated by some inadvertent action, however, the IRS *may* agree to ignore it. The result would be your corporation's continuation as a Sub S.

Important Points

When you're just starting your business or are expecting one or more loss years ahead, you may want to consider a Sub S corporation. It will give you the legal advantages of a corporation with most of the tax advantages of a partnership.

Profits and losses are allocated to owners' personal tax returns on the basis of the percentage of the business they own each day throughout the year.

If Sub S tax treatment looks like it would save you taxes—even just for a few years—you must carefully meet all the requirements set down by tax law. And you must continue to meet them in order to keep your tax-saving Sub S status.

A Sub S corporation has its limitations. In cases where you have a great deal of capital gains, the corporation may be taxed on them before they go to your own tax return. And owner-employees of a Sub S cannot be covered by the same pension and profit-sharing plans (Chapter 11) that are available through a corporation which pays regular taxes. A modified type of Keogh plan must be used ($15,000 maximum contribution in 1983; $30,000 in 1984).

But, overall, the Sub S is admirably suited for its purpose—saving you taxes in selected situations. Don't hesitate to use it.

PART FOUR

Owning Assets Can Cut Your Taxes

13

Real Estate Depreciation as a Tax Shelter

When you talk about ways to dramatically cut your taxes, depreciation of real estate has to rank near the top. By purchasing just a few rental houses, for example, the average person may be able to completely wipe out his income tax obligation to Uncle Sam for several years.

Similarly, a business can purchase and depreciate its own building or buildings. It can even acquire more real estate than it really needs, rent out part of the property to others, and depreciate it all. The deductions generated by real estate, especially in the first few years of ownership, can be surprising.

Depreciation isn't the only element of tax shelter which real estate provides. There are also deductions for interest and other carrying costs (Chapter 5). Credits for fixing up older business buildings can help eliminate your income taxes (Chapter 14). And tax law offers you special deals when you dispose of property (Chapters 17, 18, 19, 20, and 21).

Partial Defenses

Each of these tax-shelter techniques—by itself—is a partial defense against taxes. It's best to use as many of them in combination as possible each year.

Interest and other deductions help reduce your revenue so that the net earnings against which your tax rate is eventually multiplied will be lower.

Credits for the rehabilitation of business buildings arise in the year you fix up property. If you get in the habit of buying and fixing up buildings every year, you can use credits against your taxes each year.

Tax-free trades (Chapter 18) let you dispose of your property and acquire other real estate with little or no tax effect. Installment sales (Chapter 21) allow you to actually sell land or buildings with a minimum of taxes in the year of the sale. Involuntary conversion rules (Chapter 17) help you to avoid being taxed when your property is involved in a casualty. Capital gains (Chapters 19 and 20) lessen the severity of taxes on a gain you do show on your tax return.

But the single most reliable, most effective tax shelter technique for most people—one which stays with you for several years after you acquire property—is probably depreciation. It's hard to beat this deduction, especially since it is now even better than it was just a few years ago.

What Is Depreciation?

Depreciation is the process of allocating the cost or other basis of property against the revenue it produces. It is a "chipping off" of portions of the cost of an asset each year. You turn pieces of the asset into expense. Different depreciation methods allow this expensing process to move at different speeds.

Depreciation is a deduction from (shelter of) revenue. For example, the depreciation of an apartment building is a deduction from rents on the property. If depreciation, along with interest, repairs, and other deductions more than offset the structure's revenues, you have a loss. The loss can then be taken as a deduction against income you earn elsewhere (profits from your business, interest, etc.).

This is the case even though your loss is only a tax loss and is far from an actual economic loss. Although certain assets, such as buildings, increase in value, depreciation is allowed. Buildings may not "wear out," but some obsolescence does occur in subtle ways. Faucets in restrooms, kitchen appliances, and light fixtures become outmoded. More efficient heating and cooling systems are invented. All this allows buildings to be partially turned into expense each year—while they appreciate in value.

Although buildings can be depreciated, the land upon which they stand is presumed not to wear out *or* become obsolete and can't be depreciated. But certain land improvements, such as paved parking lots and sidewalks are depreciable.

Since land cannot be depreciated, you'll find yourself allocating the cost of property between land and the building which stands on it. This can normally be done by determining what fraction of value your local taxing authorities place on the land and what fraction on improvements. If they believe that three-fourths of your property's value is in the building, a $100,000 purchase price would put a $75,000 value on the part you could depreciate (the building).

Inventory is another item which cannot be depreciated. So, a rancher can depreciate his dairy or breeding livestock, but not animals he raises for sale. The owner of an office machines store can depreciate equipment he uses to run his business, but not the items he purchases for resale. A builder can depreciate his office, but not the houses he constructs for sale.

Interest-Free Loans Can Be Yours

The result of deducting as much depreciation as possible is that the taxes you'd normally pay this year are postponed. If you keep buying buildings and equipment (Chapter 15), you will continue your high depreciation deductions and put off that tax bill indefinitely—perhaps forever.

What does this do for you?

The IRS gives you an interest-free loan. You are not paying taxes when they'd otherwise be due. You are paying them years later or, perhaps, never. So, you are keeping cash to reinvest in your business. And you're not paying interest for the privilege of doing so.

Buildings You Buy Now

Buildings you acquire today, or acquired after 1980, should ordinarily be depreciated with Table A or B shown on the next two pages. For most structures, these tables yield higher depreciation than you could generate with any other allowable method.

As you can see from the tables, buildings are depreciated over a 15-year life. (If you make the purchase after February of a year, you'll have a little depreciation in the 16th year. But the result is still to turn the cost of your property into expense over 15 years.)

Table A is to be used for all depreciable real estate except low-income housing. Table B is employed to depreciate low-income housing.

Table A — All Real Estate Except Low-Income Housing

Year of Use	Percentage Applied to Unadjusted Basis (Use Column Headed by Month Building is Placed in Service)											
	Jan	Feb	Mar	Apr	May	June	July	Aug	Sept	Oct	Nov	Dec
1	12%	11%	10%	9%	8%	7%	6%	5%	4%	3%	2%	1%
2	10%	10%	11%	11%	11%	11%	11%	11%	11%	11%	11%	12%
3	9%	9%	9%	9%	10%	10%	10%	10%	10%	10%	10%	10%
4	8%	8%	8%	8%	8%	8%	9%	9%	9%	9%	9%	9%
5	7%	7%	7%	7%	7%	7%	8%	8%	8%	8%	8%	8%
6	6%	6%	6%	6%	7%	7%	7%	7%	7%	7%	7%	7%
7	6%	6%	6%	6%	6%	6%	6%	6%	6%	6%	6%	6%
8	6%	6%	6%	6%	6%	6%	5%	6%	6%	6%	6%	6%
9	6%	6%	6%	6%	5%	6%	5%	5%	5%	6%	6%	6%
10	5%	6%	5%	6%	5%	5%	5%	5%	5%	5%	6%	5%
11	5%	5%	5%	5%	5%	5%	5%	5%	5%	5%	5%	5%
12	5%	5%	5%	5%	5%	5%	5%	5%	5%	5%	5%	5%
13	5%	5%	5%	5%	5%	5%	5%	5%	5%	5%	5%	5%
14	5%	5%	5%	5%	5%	5%	5%	5%	5%	5%	5%	5%
15	5%	5%	5%	5%	5%	5%	5%	5%	5%	5%	5%	5%
16	0%	0%	1%	1%	2%	2%	3%	3%	4%	4%	4%	5%

Table B — Low-Income Housing

Year of Use	Percentage Applied to Unadjusted Basis (Use Column Headed by Month Building is Placed in Service)											
	Jan	Feb	Mar	Apr	May	June	July	Aug	Sept	Oct	Nov	Dec
1	13%	12%	11%	10%	9%	8%	7%	6%	4%	3%	2%	1%
2	12%	12%	12%	12%	12%	12%	12%	13%	13%	13%	13%	13%
3	10%	10%	10%	10%	11%	11%	11%	11%	11%	11%	11%	11%
4	9%	9%	9%	9%	9%	9%	9%	9%	10%	10%	10%	10%
5	8%	8%	8%	8%	8%	8%	8%	8%	8%	8%	8%	9%
6	7%	7%	7%	7%	7%	7%	7%	7%	7%	7%	7%	7%
7	6%	6%	6%	6%	6%	6%	6%	6%	6%	6%	6%	6%
8	5%	5%	5%	5%	5%	5%	5%	5%	5%	5%	6%	6%
9	5%	5%	5%	5%	5%	5%	5%	5%	5%	5%	5%	5%
10	5%	5%	5%	5%	5%	5%	5%	5%	5%	5%	5%	5%
11	4%	5%	5%	5%	5%	5%	5%	5%	5%	5%	5%	5%
12	4%	4%	4%	5%	4%	5%	5%	5%	5%	5%	5%	5%
13	4%	4%	4%	4%	4%	4%	5%	4%	5%	5%	5%	5%
14	4%	4%	4%	4%	4%	4%	4%	4%	4%	5%	4%	4%
15	4%	4%	4%	4%	4%	4%	4%	4%	4%	4%	4%	4%
16	0%	0%	1%	1%	2%	2%	2%	3%	3%	3%	4%	4%

Notice that the column you use in Table A or B depends upon the month in which you put the building into your business. Assume, for example, that you buy a small warehouse for your business in April of this year. You will use the column in Table A which is headed by the month "April." This means that your first year's depreciation will be nine percent; the second, 11 percent; the third, nine percent; and so on.

Let's say that you pay $70,000 for the property ($20,000 for land and $50,000 for the building which stands on the land). Since you do not depreciate land, you'll multiply the cost of the structure, $50,000, times nine percent. The result is $4,500—your depreciation deduction for the first year. Next year, you will multiply the $50,000 by 11 percent. So, next year's depreciation will be $5,500. You'll follow the April column for the entire time you own the building.

Table B (low-income housing) gives slightly more accelerated depreciation. This is because Congress wants to encourage investors to build or purchase such property. Since Table B can only be used for low-income housing, most business owners will probably never use it.

Buildings Bought Before 1981

If you still own property you bought in 1980 or earlier years, you're stuck with using one of the old methods which were allowable before January 1, 1981. In fact, you will have to continue using the method with which it was depreciated for your first year of ownership. The only change you will eventually be able to make is to switch from your present method of depreciation to the straight-line method. Because the "declining balance" depreciation methods generate a smaller deduction for each consecutive year, switching to the straight-line method late in your building's life can give larger deductions in later years of ownership.

The most accelerated method you could employ for any specific building purchased before 1981 depended upon whether you bought it new or used and whether it was residential rental property or business property.

New Rental Houses and Apartments

New residential rental real estate could be depreciated most quickly with 200 percent declining balance depreciation. This method proceeds at twice the straight-line depreciation rate and gives roughly twice the amount of deductions in the first few years that you could generate with the straight-line method.

For example, if a rental house had a 24-year remaining useful life when you bought it, straight-line depreciation would begin depreciating the property over 24 years. The 200 percent declining balance method would, in effect, start with a life of 12 years.

Used Rental Houses and Apartments

Residential rental real estate which you didn't purchase new could be legally depreciated no faster than with the 125 percent declining balance method. This method proceeds at 1.25 times the straight-line depreciation rate, giving roughly 125 percent of the deduction possible in the first few years with the straight-line rate.

New Nonresidential (Business) Real Estate

New nonresidential real estate includes new buildings which aren't rental houses or apartments. Examples are shopping centers, office buildings, warehouses, and similar properties.

Such assets bought before 1981 could be depreciated, at the most, with the 150 percent declining balance method (roughly 1.5 times the straight-line rate). If straight-line depreciation would start depreciating an asset over a 30-year life, 150 percent declining balance would start with 20 years.

Used Nonresidential (Business) Real Estate

The straight-line method was required for business buildings you bought used before 1981. This made them a poor tax shelter. The cost of the structure (less your arbitrary estimate of what you believed it would be worth at the end of its life) was deducted equally over several years.

New Components and Substantial Improvements

If you still own buildings you bought before 1981, you may be wondering how you can get additional tax shelter out of them. Fortunately, you can depreciate certain components you add to them and substantial improvements you make to them as though your expenditures were the purchase of new buildings.

Let's say that you own a small commercial building which you acquired in 1978. You were pleased with the coverage of your income the property provided in the late 1970's. But this shelter doesn't seem as nice now that you see other people buying buildings today and drawing big new depreciation deductions from them with Tables A and B.

You could buy other properties. But you also have another option.

Tax law will apparently let you add a component such as a carport, a central heating system, or others, and depreciate the component as if it were a building you bought in 1981 or later years. You can use Table A with its accelerated depreciation method and shorter life.

Similarly, a "substantial improvement" can be made to a building you own and the costs of this remodeling depreciated as though they were employed to buy a new property. A "substantial improvement" is one which costs at least one-fourth of what you paid for the property you're now improving. (Certain adjustments may require a slightly higher or lower cost.)

Assume that you own a 15-year-old business building which would be worth considerably more after remodeling. Let us say you paid $80,000 for it. If so, you'll probably have to spend at least $20,000 on improvements in order to get this special deal.

If you do not want to put that much money into improvements for this particular property, you can instead use your cash to buy another building. Since you're making the purchase now, rather than before 1981, you can use Table A to depreciate it rapidly.

Any building which you decide to substantially improve can be as little as three years old, but typically will probably be older. The changes must be finished within 24 months of the time you start them. The IRS does not want a continuing program of repair to eventually be called a "substantial improvement."

Substantial Rehabilitation

In some cases, it is possible to claim either a "substantial improvement" *or* a "substantial rehabilitation" for fixing up an older building. You can use Table A to quickly depreciate a substantial *improvement* of your business property. But you can get a tax credit to directly reduce your taxes with a substantial *rehabilitation* (Chapter 14).

To take a tax credit for a substantial rehabilitation, the structure must be at least 30 years old. If it's 40 or more, the credit is even higher.

The changes which qualify for substantial rehabilitation are more restrictive than those which qualify as substantial improvements. Enlargements aren't eligible. At least 75 percent of the existing outside walls must remain outside walls.

Most rehabilitations must also normally be completed within 24 months of the time they start. However, if all remodeling is done under a set of architectural plans and specifications, the IRS may allow you up to a total of five years for the work.

Although roughly one-quarter of the cost of a building must be spent to have a substantial improvement, the spending requirement for a rehabilitation is different. You must spend more than the cost or adjusted basis of the property. "Adjusted basis" is often cost minus the total of depreciation deductions you've taken on the property since you bought it. If you've owned a building for several years, the depreciation you have deducted may reduce its cost to a surprisingly low adjusted basis. In any case, tax law requires you to spend more than $5,000.

For example, let's say that you bought a used warehouse for $54,000 about 15 years ago. The building (35 years old) may now be worth $150,000, but this figure is irrelevant. What you are looking for is your adjusted basis.

Assuming you have taken a total of $28,000 of depreciation deductions on it, your adjusted basis for the property would now be $26,000 ($54,000 cost, less $28,000 of depreciation taken). So, you must spend only $26,001 or more to qualify for generous tax credits under the substantial rehabilitation rules.

In addition to cutting your taxes with the credit, you will be able to depreciate most of the cost of your rehabilitation. Although you will probably have to use straight-line depreciation instead of the rapid deductions allowed by Table A, this depreciation will add to the tax shelter your business badly needs.

Which Is Better: Improvement or Rehabilitation?

Let's assume that you buy a 32-year-old building for which both a substantial improvement and a substantial rehabilitation are possible. Which would give you better tax shelter?

Figuring you can spend $50,000 and qualify for either one, your first 15 years of ownership might give you the tax savings shown in Table C (if you're in the 40 percent tax bracket).

Table C — Tax Benefits of Improvement Vs. Rehabilitation

	Substantial Improvement			Substantial Rehabilitation		
Year	Tax Credit	Depre-ciation Deduction	Accum. Tax Savings	Tax Credit	Depre-ciation Deduction	Accum. Tax Savings
1	$-0-	$6,000	$ 2,400	$4,500	$3,033	$ 5,713
2		5,000	4,400		3,033	6,926
3		4,500	6,200		3,033	8,139
4		4,000	7,800		3,033	9,352
5		3,500	9,200		3,033	10,565
6		3,000	10,400		3,033	11,778
7		3,000	11,600		3,033	12,991
8		3,000	12,800		3,033	14,204
9		3,000	14,000		3,033	15,417
10		2,500	15,000		3,033	16,630
11		2,500	16,000		3,033	17,843
12		2,500	17,000		3,033	19,056
13		2,500	18,000		3,033	20,269
14		2,500	19,000		3,033	21,482
15		2,500	20,000		3,033	22,700
Total Tax Savings			20,000			22,700

As you can see, you're much farther ahead in the first year or two with a substantial rehabilitation. In the example shown in Table C, your tax credit and depreciation deduction with the rehabilitation would give you an accumulated total tax savings at the end of the first year of $5,713. This compares to a $2,400 savings with an improvement. The second year would bring the totals up to $6,926 and $4,400 respectively.

And your tax shelter (accumulated tax savings) is better across the entire estimated life of the remodeling job, assuming you depreciate it over 15 years. This is because you get a big tax-saving credit in the year you do a rehabilitation, then are still able to deduct most of the depreciation you'd get with a substantial improvement.

Trade or Refinance, Don't Sell

When you dispose of property, be extremely careful how you go about it. Too many people assume that they will automatically have a long-term capital gain (taxed lightly) if they sell a building. This may not be true at all. The gain on a sale *could* be taxed severely.

Trading your property for other business or investment real estate (Chapter 18) or refinancing your property in order to raise cash for another purchase can often result in much less tax than you'd owe if you sold your real estate. Trading may require more effort than selling, and refinancing may not raise as much cash, but the potential tax savings can make them both worth your careful consideration.

If you cannot see any alternative to selling your property, at least take time to consider using the installment sales method (Chapter 21). It could help you pay your tax bill over a period of several years instead of owing all of it in the year of the sale.

Important Points

Tax shelter potential should not be the only reason why you buy real estate. Other factors such as possible increase in the property's value, an improvement in your business' location, and the goals you've set for expansion of your business are also important.

But depreciation deductions should always be considered when you make a decision to purchase or not to purchase a building. Coverage of your income is important if you want to reinvest earnings. The less tax you pay today, the less you'll need to borrow from banks to finance your business' growth, and the faster your net worth will increase.

Maximum depreciation deductions will give you the nearest thing there is to an interest-free loan from Uncle Sam. The IRS helps you to build your business by allowing you to keep more cash with which to operate your enterprise.

Depreciation deductions are especially liberal on buildings you acquire after 1980. Although a structure bought in 1980 or earlier years might have been depreciated over a useful life of 30 or more years, Tables A and B allow you to depreciate one you acquire now over only 15 years. And your depreciation method today may be more accelerated than the one for which you would have been eligible earlier.

If you still own a building which you began depreciating before 1981, you're stuck with the old methods of figuring the deduction. Your only hopes for squeezing extra tax shelter out of the property are to add components, do substantial improvements, or carry out a substantial rehabilitation. At least these changes to your structure can add to the depreciation you are already deducting. And a rehabilitation can also cut your taxes directly with a generous credit.

When you want to dispose of property, give some thought to the taxes which will result. You'll usually find that an outright sale for cash will cause a larger tax bill than you think. A tax-free trade, refinancing, or an installment sale may give you a considerably lower tax liability.

Saving taxes isn't a single battle. It is an extended campaign. You cannot expect to use an occasional tax break and save nearly as much as if you use every loophole you can get your hands on.

That is what saving taxes by owning buildings is all about—using every tax-cutting technique available, from tax-free trades to substantial rehabilitations to rapid depreciation.

After all, while you are putting in your best effort to maximize your business profits for the year, the IRS is waiting patiently at your door to take part of those earnings. You've got to take advantage of tax breaks to protect as much of those profits as you can.

If you let them, buildings can save you taxes each day of every year.

14

Tax Credits for Rehabilitating Your Building

Recent years have seen changes in income tax rules which make the tax-shelter potential of buildings better than it ever has been. Structures can be depreciated over shorter lives than ever before and many types of buildings can be depreciated with more rapid depreciation (Chapter 13). In addition, a liberal credit is allowed for the cost of rehabilitating business buildings.

Let's say, for example, that you need $50,000 to remodel a building you own. All you have is $10,000 cash and every cent of it is earmarked to pay your taxes for the year.

Is there an alternative?

Sure. Just borrow $40,000 to go with your $10,000. Spend $50,000 fixing up the building. Doing this may completely wipe out your tax bill. What you'd otherwise pay in taxes goes into making your property more valuable. In addition to this immediate benefit, you will gain a long-term tax-saving advantage by depreciating the improvements over several years.

This may sound too good to be true, but it isn't. It is part of Congress' plan to protect and revitalize the country's vast inventory of older buildings. The word "older" here means only 30 or more years old—which includes a wide selection of serviceable structures.

You may already own one or more properties which fit this description. Or you may be considering the purchase of a building for

business use or to own as an investment. If so, this credit could assist
you in making your choice from among available properties.

Why a Credit Is Better

As you've seen, a deduction reduces the income against which tax
rates are multiplied. But a credit cuts taxes dollar for dollar after they
are already figured. So, a credit will act as a direct reduction of your
tax bill.

That's how, in the example above, your expenditure of only
$50,000 was able to cut your tax bill immediately by $10,000—the
credit from your work was $10,000. If you'd had a $10,000 deduction,
instead of a credit, your taxable income would have been lowered by
$10,000. Your tax savings would have been some percentage of the
$10,000 reduction ($3,500, if you were in the 35 percent tax bracket).

Choose Your Percentage

Actually, the credit for $50,000 of fixing-up expenditures isn't
always $10,000 (20 percent of the $50,000). For buildings constructed
between 30 and 40 years ago, the credit is 15 percent of rehabilitation
costs. They must be 40 or more years old in order for you to get the
full 20 percent as your credit.

This means that, for example, $40,000 of remodeling costs put
into a 35-year-old building would cut your taxes by 15 percent of the
$40,000, or $6,000. If the property were 40 years old, you'd get 20
percent of the $40,000, or $8,000, taken off your tax bill.

In some situations, it may be worthwhile to wait a year or two
before you start the work. Let's say that your structure is 39 years old.
Waiting one more year would raise it to age 40 and entitle you to 20
percent instead of 15 percent as your credit. If your remodeling costs
amount to $40,000 your patience in waiting the extra year would raise
your credit $2,000 (from $6,000 to $8,000).

"Qualified" Rehabilitation

If it's going to hand out this type of tax-saving possibilities to business owners and investors, tax law figures that it can attach a few requirements. And, in many cases, the requirements are not unreasonable.

Amount to Spend

The first thing the IRS wants to be sure of is that the rehabilitation is "substantial." This means that what you spend for remodeling must be larger than your cost of or adjusted basis—usually cost minus accumulated depreciation—in the building. (If you have owned and depreciated a building for several years, your adjusted basis may be considerably less than what you paid for the property. Your accountant can give you an exact figure.)

Assume, for instance, that you bought a building 10 years ago for $45,000 and that you've taken $25,000 of depreciation on it in that time. Your adjusted basis is now $20,000 ($45,000, less $25,000). Your remodeling will need to cost at least $20,001.

Whatever you find you must spend to qualify for a "substantial" rehabilitation, the cost must be more than $5,000. This is the absolute minimum.

If you are presently trying to choose the best of several buildings for your business or as an investment, the spending requirement may help you to make the decision. To earn the credit, you'll need to spend at least as much as the building's cost. This may direct you to a structure in an older neighborhood which is coming back into popularity.

Of course, many older buildings are located in slums which will remain slums for the foreseeable future. Your remodeling dollars would be wasted in such a location, because they'd improve the property beyond its highest and best use. You would not be able to recover your investment by selling.

But many cities and towns have older neighborhoods which either are still desirable or are coming back into style. These are areas where you can often substantially increase the value of a property by rehabilitating it and, at the same time, substantially cut your income taxes.

Your remodeling can take place across a two-year period. In fact, if it's done under a complete set of architectural plans for the entire job, you can take up to five years to complete the work.

Type of Work to Do

The credit can be taken on rehabilitation. Very little new construction will qualify. At least 75 percent of the external walls of your building must stay in place as external walls. Enlargements of your structure won't qualify. You cannot take the credit on the purchase price of a building. And constructing or completing a new building is out of the question.

Except for historic structures, no work can be done on rental houses or apartments. Only rehabilitation of business buildings qualifies.

This tax law was passed simply to encourage people to fix up older business buildings. Anything else probably won't be eligible for the credit—even though you may be able to get plenty of depreciation deductions out of it.

Historic Structures

Care must be exercised if you plan to remodel an historic building or one which is located in an historical district. Special interest groups have caused different rules to apply in these cases.

The good news is that your credit is 25 percent instead of 15 or 20 percent. And the rehabilitation of residential structures, instead of just business buildings, qualifies for the credit.

But your rehabilitation must be "certified" by the Secretary of the Interior as being appropriate for the building. Your remodeling efforts must take into account the "historic character" of the building or the district around it.

Improvements by Tenants

One part of the new rules can benefit both owners of business buildings and their tenants. If a landlord prefers not to fix up his property or doesn't have the resources to do so, the lessee can take the credit by paying for the work himself. In order for the lessee to qualify for the credit, his lease must extend at least 15 years beyond the day that remodeling is completed.

In the case of improvements by a tenant—whether the tenant gets a credit or not—the property's owner can get a real bonus.

When rent is reduced or waived to encourage the tenant to make improvements to the property, the owner is taxed on the value of any rehabilitation. The IRS figures that the improvements are taking the place of rent. Rent is taxable. So, anything that takes its place is taxed.

But, if rehabilitation is done by the tenant without a reduction of rent, the remodeling is tax-free to the building's owner.

For example, assume that you own a building to which a tenant wants to make improvements. You approve the alterations and your tenant makes them while paying his regular rent. You're not taxed when he does the remodeling.

If you have an appropriate voice in the type of changes to be made, this can work out very well for you. You get the remodeling you want at no cost and the tenant acts as general contractor. You're removed from hassles with subcontractors and city inspectors, changes in weather and other problems.

Depreciation Disadvantages

Although you will be able to take a credit now for rehabilitating property *and* save taxes in later years by depreciating your rehabilitation expenditures, you'll have two disadvantages.

First of all, you must subtract your tax credit (½ the credit for historic property) from the cost of your rehabilitation. The remainder is what you may depreciate. If you get a $10,000 credit for $50,000 of rehabilitation expenditures you can only depreciate $40,000 of them ($50,000 cost, less $10,000 credit).

In addition, you will have to use straight-line depreciation on these fix-up costs, instead of the more rapid methods explained in Chapter 13. The straight-line method gives you basically the same deductions in total. It simply does not give them to you as soon as do the accelerated methods.

Most people will find that they are better off to accept these two limitations and take the credit anyway. There is hardly anything which can take the place of a $6,000, $10,000, or $25,000 immediate cut in your tax bill. As long as you'll also be able to take almost the same total depreciation deductions (even if more slowly), you cannot help improving your tax situation.

Loans Build Your Tax-Saving Potential

Loans can help build up your tax credit for the year. You may have only $5,000 or $10,000 in cash. But using this as equity in a rehabilitation can substantially cut your taxes.

Consider spending $100,000 to remodel one or more business buildings during a year. At the 15 to 20 percent credit level, you're saving $15,000 to $20,000 in income taxes. If you have enough equity in buildings you presently own or can generate enough earnings from your business to finance several rehabilitations, you may be able to completely wipe out your tax bill year after year. You'll be investing your tax dollars in your properties instead of in the IRS.

Interest rates may be high. But the flip side of high interest is high deductions. Whatever rate of interest you pay, you will likely be able to deduct it on your tax return.

Important Points

Congress is finally becoming serious about encouraging people to preserve this nation's wealth of older buildings. The credit for fixing them up may go a long way toward retaining and improving the usefulness of numerous structures.

And, for the business owner or investor who'd rather put his cash into remodeling than into income taxes, it is a perfect opportunity to do so. All he's got to do is to make improvements according to the rules which will allow his credit.

You may already own a building which is ripe for rehabilitation. Or you may be thinking about buying one or more which need work. If there is an older area of your city which is coming back into popularity, there isn't much reason to complain about high income taxes—not when you can wipe them out with this credit.

But choose your neighborhoods carefully. Do not spend so much to remodel a building that you couldn't get your money out of it if you sold it. Some areas simply cannot justify improvements. They are declining in value, instead of appreciating.

Be sure to plan in advance every element of fixing up a building— from exactly which improvements you'll make, to how much you will need to borrow, to the exact length of time the work will take. With this kind of tax savings at stake, you do not want any mistakes to be made.

Every property owner's tax situation is different. For the size of tax savings which is possible with the rehabilitation credit, a short visit to your tax advisor should be a part of the planning process. His modest fee ought to be dwarfed by your tax savings and his advice could protect you from traps and help you reduce your tax bill even more than you had figured.

15

Depreciating Vehicles, Furniture, and Equipment

In Chapter 13, you saw how real estate depreciation could provide shelter to protect your income from taxes. Vehicles, furniture, equipment, and other business personal property can do the same.

The phrase "business personal property" may seem to be a contradiction. But it isn't. The word "personal" just refers to the fact that the asset is not real estate. Equipment, livestock, cranes, cars, trucks, and similar items not attached to land are "personal" property.

In order to be depreciated, of course, an asset has to be used in your business. You can't depreciate the car your spouse uses for shopping and errands or the calculator your children use to do their homework.

Similarly, it is not possible to depreciate inventory—those items you hold for resale. You can only depreciate assets you intend to employ in business operations over a period of time.

New Expensing Breakthrough

One of the best tax breaks for small businesses to come along in years is one which allows you to expense part of the cost of tangible personal property you buy in 1982 or later years.

The word "tangible" points out those items which have a physical existence—not copyrights, patents, trademarks, or others which are represented only by a piece of paper.

Instead of depreciating such assets over a period of several years, you can simply deduct them on your tax return (with limits) in the year you buy them. The maximum cost of tangible personal property that you can deduct on your tax return each year is as follows:

Year	Amount You Can Deduct
1982	$ 5,000
1983	5,000
1984	7,500
1985	7,500
1986 and later years	10,000

If you buy more than the limit for a year, you can deduct in that year the cost of assets up to your limit. Your purchases above the limit can then be depreciated with the regular depreciation tables.

So, if you buy $20,000 of equipment and vehicles during 1984, you can deduct the first $7,500. The remaining $12,500 of cost ($20,000, less $7,500) would be depreciated with the tables.

One disadvantage of deducting the cost of assets, instead of depreciating that cost, is that you can't take investment credit (Chapter 16) on the part you deduct. Deducting the cost of an asset will usually cut more taxes in the year you acquire it. But across the entire life of an asset, the combination of investment credit and regular depreciation may be able to save you more taxes in total.

For example, your investment credit on $20,000 of property would be at least $1,200 and possibly as much as $2,000. This would be a direct, dollar-for-dollar reduction of your taxes that you would get in addition to depreciation deductions.

Deducting $7,500 (of your $20,000) of purchases when you acquire them, rather than depreciating that $7,500 across the next several years would limit your investment credit to a percentage of the other $12,500 of equipment and vehicles. So, your investment credit would be only $750 to $1,250.

	Taking $7,500 Early Deduction	Using Only Regular Depreciation
Your Total Investment Credit	$750 to $1,250	$1,200 to $2,000
Your Total Deductions (including year of purchase)	$20,000	$20,000

You'll just have to look at your tax situation each year to see whether you need to dramatically cut your taxes that year, or whether you can forego expensing the cost of assets you acquire in order to generate a larger investment credit.

How the Tables Work

As with real estate, tangible personal property you put into business service in 1981 and later years is depreciated with the help of tables. If it was used in your business in 1980 or earlier, an asset can only be depreciated today with one of the old methods.

Table A is employed for cars and light-duty trucks you buy now. Table B is used for most other types of tangible personal property you acquire today.

Other tables supplied by the IRS help you depreciate railroad tank cars, theme park structures, mobile homes, public utility property, certain coal burners and boilers, and a few other selected items.

Table A — Cars and Light-Duty Trucks

	Percentage Applied to Unadjusted Basis
Year of Use	Asset Put Into Use January 1, 1981 or Later
1	25%
2	38%
3	37%

Table B — Most Tangible Personal Property

	Percentage Applied to Unadjusted Basis
Year of Use	Asset Put Into Use January 1, 1981 or Later
1	15%
2	22%
3	21%
4	21%
5	21%

The percentage you choose is multiplied by the cost of your asset. Assume, for example, that you purchase a business pickup truck in 1984 for $10,000. The percentage to be multiplied by its cost each year would yield depreciation deductions as follows:

Year	Table A Percent		Cost		Annual Deduction
1984	25%	×	$10,000	=	$2,500
1985	38%	×	$10,000	=	$3,800
1986	37%	×	$10,000	=	$3,700

If you bought a $10,000 computer (Table B) in 1986, the depreciation deductions over its life would appear as follows:

Year	Table B Percent		Cost		Annual Deduction
1986	15%	×	$10,000	=	$1,500
1987	22%	×	$10,000	=	$2,200
1988	21%	×	$10,000	=	$2,100
1989	21%	×	$10,000	=	$2,100
1990	21%	×	$10,000	=	$2,100

You depreciate an asset by its full first year's percentage whether you make the purchase early or late in a year. For example, if you buy a $10,000 business car on January 2, 1983, or December 31, 1983, your depreciation comes out the same—25 percent of $10,000 (Table A).

This fact can enable you to generate deductions late in a year with little cash outlay. If you buy the $10,000 business car with a $1,000 down payment, for instance, your $1,000 investment will yield a $2,500 deduction for the year. While it will reduce your depreciation to 97 percent of these figures (95 percent for assets other than vehicles), you'll be able to take a $600 investment credit as a direct reduction of your taxes for the year of purchase

Assuming that you are in the 40 percent tax bracket, a $2,425 depreciation deduction (97 percent of $2,500) and a $600 tax credit would save you about $1,600 of taxes in the year you buy the automobile—a $1,600 tax savings with a $1,000 investment.

Assets Bought Before 1981

On the other hand, tangible personal property you put into business use before the first day of 1981 will continue to be depreciated with one of the old methods. You're stuck with it for the life of the property.

New Tangible Personal Business Property

Property you bought new in 1980 and earlier years could normally be depreciated with the 200 percent declining balance method of depreciation. The first year or so of depreciation with this method was about double the deduction yielded by straight-line depreciation.

Used Tangible Personal Business Property

If the property you purchased in 1980 or earlier years was not new when you acquired it, you were limited to the 150 percent declining balance method of depreciation. Your depreciation for the first year or two was roughly 1.5 times the deduction you could have had with the straight-line method of depreciation.

Straight-Line Depreciation

Certain assets you put into service before 1981 had to be depreciated with the straight-line method. These primarily were items which weren't going to last at least three years beyond the date you acquired them and intangible assets such as patents and copyrights.

Straight-line depreciation spreads the cost of property equally over the life you estimate for it and allows approximately equal deductions each year.

Even today, if you expect losses this year but anticipate profits later on, you can choose to depreciate assets you purchase with the straight-line method. This will push part of what you could deduct now into those later years.

Trade, Don't Sell

As you saw in Chapter 13, tax law allows you to shelter as much income with depreciation as you can. But when you sell a building, part or all of the gain may be turned into the same type of income which was sheltered. The result is that part of the gain on a sale may be unprotected ordinary income like net profits, commissions, or interest—rather than long-term capital gain.

The same result is seen when you sell tangible personal business property. In fact, you're even more likely to see gain turned into ordinary income when you sell vehicles, furniture, equipment, or other personal property you've depreciated.

The tax-free trade (Chapter 18) can partly or completely steer you clear of this problem. Such trades are usually far easier to arrange for tangible personal property than they are for real estate. It is simpler to swap a pickup for a pickup or an adding machine for a calculator than it is to exchange a warehouse for a shopping center.

But, if you aren't able to trade your property away, you can still minimize your taxes for the year of the sale by selling the item with the installment sales method (Chapter 21). This will keep your taxes on the sale from being due until payments are made. In this way, your tax bill can often be spread out over several years.

Important Points

As long as you're going to need tangible personal property in order to run your business, you might as well squeeze all the tax shelter out of it that you can. This means taking the investment credit (Chapter 16) on anything you can and being sure that your depreciation deduction is as high as it should be.

Expensing part or all of the cost of an asset in the year you acquire it can build up your deductions quickly. If you need deductions badly and prefer to let each of the next years take care of itself, this option can be very attractive. However, you will be limited on the amount of investment credit you can take for the year.

Depreciation for items you buy today is fairly standardized. You'll usually employ Table A or B—letting the year in which you put the asset into business use determine how rapidly it will be depreciated.

If you're still depreciating property you brought into the business in 1980 or earlier years, you must continue using one of the older methods. Whether the item was new or used when you purchased it probably still determines the method by which it is depreciated.

As with buildings, you should be extremely careful about disposing of tangible personal business property. A sale for cash could cause a severe tax result. When possible, consider a tax-free trade. If a trade cannot be arranged, an installment sale may at least postpone your taxes to the years in which you receive payments.

Tangible personal business property may not offer the potential tax shelter you can find in real estate. But a good tax-saving program must take advantage of every loophole available to your business. And properly depreciating equipment, furniture, vehicles, and other similar items can help you reduce your tax bill each year.

16

Extra Cash with Investment Credit

Most businesses must own a certain amount of equipment—desks, typewriters, computers, cars, trucks, cranes, airplanes, and others. You can cut your taxes in the year you buy these, not only with depreciation, but also with investment credit.

The investment credit was placed in tax law to encourage business owners to buy equipment. Congress figured that if people would purchase equipment, the economy would be stimulated and unemployment would be low.

A "credit" is a direct reduction of taxes, as opposed to a deduction, which lowers income before taxes are computed. A $100 deduction will cause your taxable income to be $100 less, and might reduce your taxes by $30 if you're in the 30 percent tax bracket. But a $100 credit will cut your taxes by $100.

The differing effects of a deduction and a credit on your tax return might be compared as follows:

	Deduction	Credit
Revenue	$1,000	$1,000
Less: Deduction	100	-0-
Taxable Income	$ 900	$1,000
Tax Rate	× .30	× .30
Taxes	$ 270	$ 300
Less: Credit	-0-	100
Taxes Due	$ 270	$ 200

Naturally, saving taxes should not be the reason why you buy equipment. Almost all equipment you acquire will immediately begin to decline in value. So, only needed items should be bought.

But this credit is an ideal way for you to plan acquisitions of equipment so that taxes can be reduced when you choose. Even if you take advantage of this tax-saving technique, your depreciation deductions usually won't be seriously affected. So, people who buy equipment and forget to take the credit are literally throwing away cash.

Which Items Are Eligible?

Purchases and certain leases of tangible personal property qualify for investment credit. These include such items as trucks, cars, calculators, desks, furniture, airplanes, saws, and other equiment. Livestock (except for horses) which you buy for dairy or breeding purposes are usually eligible.

You normally can't take the credit on land or buildings. But it is allowed on certain farm buildings. And you can take a slightly different credit for remodeling business buildings (Chapter 14).

The investment credit cannot be taken on the inventory of your business. For example, let's say that you are in the office equipment business. The inventory of equipment you buy and sell is not eligible for the credit. But a calculator you use to figure invoices *would* be, as would the desk where you sit. These are used in your business, not held for resale.

An asset on which you take investment credit can be new or used when you buy it. But you cannot take the credit on the cost of more than $125,000 of used property in any one year ($150,000 in 1985 and later years).

Assume, for example, that you buy $175,000 of used equipment in 1984. You'll be able to take investment credit on $125,000 of it. No credit will be allowed on the other $50,000.

Amount of the Credit

The investment credit is six percent of the cost of cars and light-duty trucks and 10 percent of the cost of most other eligible property.

Let's say that you purchase a $10,000 car for your business. Six percent of its $10,000 cost, or $600, is your credit—a direct reduction of your taxes in the year of purchase. Although no credit is allowed on the car in subsequent years, you can depreciate it in the first and later years. This rapid depreciation (Chapter 15) can help save taxes in each year the deduction is allowed.

Assume, also, that you buy $30,000 of other equipment in the same year. If none of these items is a car or light-duty truck, your credit will be 10 percent of $30,000, or $3,000. This $3,000 will be another direct reduction of your taxes.

In addition to regular equipment and certain livestock, farmers can take 10 percent credit on the cost of single-purpose farm buildings. These are structures which are built for the specific purpose of raising one type of animal or plant.

Although farmers get a good deal, people who own rental houses and apartments are treated poorly. Items otherwise eligible for investment credit (appliances, furniture, and others) lose their eligibility when placed in premises where people live.

Equipment such as ladders, painting machinery, cars, and similar property used *around* rental houses and apartments are usually eligible for the credit. Also, coin-operated machinery which is located on the property (and made available to both people who live there and those who don't) is usually acceptable.

If you are leasing, rather than purchasing, new equipment, you may be able to take part or all of the credit you'd get if you bought the property. Besides the consent of the asset's owner, your credit can depend upon the life of the property, the length of the lease, and the type of lease.

The Limits Are High

The total amount of investment credit you can use to cut your taxes in any single year will depend on both the amount of credit you generate and your total tax bill for the year. Most people are not likely to reach the annual limits. If you do, you may find yourself using part of one year's credit to cut your taxes in prior years and later years.

1) If your taxes total $25,000 or less for the year, you can use all of your credit up to the amount of your taxes. For example, if your credit turns out to be $8,000, and your taxes are $10,000, you can wipe out $8,000 of taxes and pay only $2,000 to the IRS.

Your Tax Bill	$10,000
Less: Your Credit	8,000
What You Have to Pay	$ 2,000

If the credit is $8,000 and your taxes are only $5,000, you wipe out your tax bill this year, and have a $3,000 credit to use to reduce taxes you paid in the last three years or will owe in the next 15 years.

Your Tax Bill	$ 5,000
Less: Your Credit	8,000
What You Have to Pay	$ -0-
Credit to be Used in Other Years	$ 3,000

2) If the credit is more than $25,000, but your taxes are less, you can wipe out your taxes and carry the remaining credit back three years or over to the next 15 years. Assume, for example, that your credit is $28,000, but your tax bill is only $12,000. You can probably entirely offset this year's taxes and carry the remaining $16,000 back or over to offset the taxes of other years.

Your Tax Bill	$12,000
Less: Your Credit	28,000
What You Have to Pay	$ -0-
Credit to be Used in Other Years	$16,000

3) When both your credit and taxes are over $25,000, the credit which can be used in a single year is limited. The limit for 1983 and later years is the first $25,000 of taxes, plus 85 percent of the remainder.

For instance, if your investment credit in 1983 is $40,000 and your taxes are $30,000, you can wipe out the first $25,000 of tax liability without trouble. After that, you are limited to 85 percent of the remaining $5,000 of taxes ($30,000 total taxes, less $25,000). Since 85 percent of $5,000 s $4,250, you can offset $29,250 of taxes for the year ($25,000 plus $4,250).

Tax Bill for the Year	$30,000
First $25,000	25,000
Excess Above $25,000	$ 5,000
	× .85
Portion Allowed Above First $25,000	$ 4,250
First $25,000	$25,000
Portion Allowed Above First $25,000	$ 4,250
Total Credit You Can Use This Year	$29,250

Since your total credit in this example is $40,000 but you can only use $29,250 this leaves $10,750 to offset against taxes in previous years or future years.

Fortunately, most businesses don't need to worry about reaching these limits. If none of the equipment you purchase during a single year is cars or light-duty trucks, you'd have to buy $250,000 worth before the first limit ($25,000) would be reached. Even if you reach the limit in a year, your credit is not lost, but is merely used in more than one year.

Planning Your Taxes During Inflation

Planning your taxes is always important regardless of current economic conditions. But it is especially critical during inflation. The investment credit for purchases of equipment can provide badly needed cash to help your business acquire additional assets, pay bills, or meet other requirements.

Whether you make the purchase in January or December of a year, you get the full six or ten percent of your investment as a credit. If you are planning to buy an item in either December of 19A or January of the next year (19B), you should seriously consider a December, 19A purchase. When you buy in December of 19A, the credit lowers your taxes for 19A. Your tax savings can then be used for whatever purpose you choose—even the down payment on the item bought.

If you wait to buy until January of 19B, your final tax savings won't be received until the end of 19B. So, even though the purchase is made only one month earlier, buying in December of 19A will give you your tax savings a full year earlier.

If You Use the Expensing Option

As you saw in Chapter 15, you can expense (and deduct) the first $5,000, $7,500, or $10,000 of equipment you buy during each year, rather than depreciating it over several years. If you do so, you can't take investment credit on the portion you expense.

Unless you are badly in need of deductions in the year you buy property, you might consider taking the investment credit and depreciating the item over several years with regular depreciation methods. Your total depreciation is about the same (although taken later) *and* you can take investment credit. So, your *total* tax breaks are greater.

For example, buying a $7,500 computer and expensing it could get you a commendable $7,500 deduction for the year of purchase. If you need lots of deductions now, this may be the way to go.

But, if you can find other deductions for the current year, you could depreciate the cost of the computer over several years (Chapter 15). Doing this would allow you to also take investment credit on it. Even though you'd find yourself deducting depreciation over several years instead of one, you get both depreciation and credit.

Be Careful About Selling Assets

Selling a car or truck less than three years after you buy it can cause part of the credit you took in the year of purchase to be added to your taxes in the year of the sale. For most other equipment, selling the item less than five years after acquisition will cause the same problem.

You'll notice that part of the credit which was taken is *added* to your tax bill. Since investment credit is subtracted directly from your taxes, disposing of property early causes the reverse to happen.

Assume, for instance, that you buy a $30,000 airplane and take $3,000 of credit in the year of purchase. After two years, you decide to sell it. You are required to add about $1,800 to your tax bill in the year of sale. You're still $1,200 better off ($3,000, less $1,800) than if you had not taken the credit. But, if you sell without thinking about it, this addition to your tax bill can be quite a surprise.

Important Points

Service, merchandising, and manufacturing enterprises all need equipment in order to do business. Fortunately, tax law allows a generous reduction of taxes in the year you buy property which is eligible for the investment credit.

Some businesses, especially farming, are treated even more liberally than average. Others, such as the ownership of residential rental property, are restricted in the type of assets they can purchase with the credit in mind.

Although most smaller businesses never reach the annual limits tax law puts on the amount of credit which can be used, some companies do. They acquire more than $125,000 (or $150,000) of used assets and/or purchase a large amount of new property, then find themselves carrying investment credit back to earlier years or forward to later ones. There's certainly nothing wrong with this as long as the credit is used to save taxes.

Whatever equipment you buy, do *not* (as many people do) forget to take the investment credit. If you did neglect to take the credit in any of the last three years, you can probably file an amended tax return in order to get a refund of part of what you paid the IRS.

You owe it to your business and to yourself, especially during inflation, to pay out as little cash as possible for taxes. The investment credit was set up with exactly this in mind. It's a tax-saving gift from tax law to you.

PART FIVE

Low-Tax Disposals of Assets

17

Saving Taxes with Involuntary Conversions

Most businesses, at one time or another, experience thefts, hail or wind damage, fires, condemnations and all other manner of unexpected, unusual, or sudden events.

The result of a theft or casualty may be a loss which is deductible on your tax return (Chapter 3). On the other hand, insurance, scrap value, recovery from a suit in court, and other compensation may give you a gain as a result of the incident.

You say it doesn't sound possible that you could have a gain on a theft or casualty?

When the total compensation you receive is more than the cost or other basis of the item lost, or more than the decline in fair market value because of the casualty, the result *is* probably a gain.

Of course, you didn't ask for a theft or casualty. You did not want the gain. Yet you will have a taxable gain placed on your tax return unless you take specific steps.

And the problem is even more severe than you imagine. You might think that if the amounts received as compensation for loss of property are less than the asset's value, the result is a loss. This is not necessarily true.

Let's assume, for example, that you own an acre of land which your city condemns. The city wants to build a street across it. You paid $20,000 for the property, but it's worth $30,000 at the time it is condemned. If the city pays $28,000 for the property, an $8,000 gain results (not a $2,000 loss). If the city pays $34,000, you have a $14,000 gain (not a $4,000 gain). Gain is calculated by looking at the cost or other basis of the property ($20,000), not at its current market value ($30,000). In this particular case, you'll have a loss only if the city pays you less than $20,000. An $18,000 settlement would give you a $2,000 loss.

Condemnation Award	$28,000	$34,000	$18,000
Cost or Other Basis	20,000	20,000	20,000
Gain (Loss)	$ 8,000	$14,000	($ 2,000)

Thus, you can 1) be disappointed when your property is harmed or taken from you, 2) receive less insurance or other proceeds than it is worth, and 3) again be upset when you owe a tax bill for which you never asked.

But the third problem can be prevented.

Keeping Gains From Being Taxed

When you actually have a loss from a theft, condemnation, or casualty, it isn't postponed. It is deducted on your tax return for the year it happens. Few people would want to put off taking a deduction anyway, so this works out well. If you lost your land to the city for $18,000 in the example above, your $2,000 loss would go to your tax return in the year of condemnation.

Gains, however, are a different matter. Few people would voluntarily choose to be taxed on a gain caused by something beyond their control. Fortunately, involuntary conversion rules give four steps which can keep gains from being taxed:

1) Spend the entire proceeds you receive on another asset;

2) Make sure the replacement you buy is the right type of property;

3) Acquire your replacement within the time allowed; and

4) Tell the IRS that you want to postpone any gain.

Taking any three of these steps without the fourth is of no use. All four steps must be properly followed before the gain can be postponed.

Reinvesting Enough

Tax law wants you to buy replacement property costing at least as much as the insurance proceeds or other compensation you receive. If you do this, you're showing that you really wanted to keep the property you lost. If you do not spend at least that much, the law sees you as "cashing in" part of your investment as though you did not need or want all of it.

In the last part of our example above, you had a $2,000 loss. Reinvesting any amount in another piece of land, of course, won't prevent you from placing the loss on your tax return. Losses are not postponed.

To postpone a gain, however, the insurance or other proceeds *must* be reinvested. If you want to keep all gain off your tax return, the replacement property must cost at least as much as the total you receive from insurance, condemnation payments, and all other proceeds. If you reinvest less than this total, part or all of your gain will be taxed.

Reinvesting too little won't necessarily cause *all* of the gain to be taxed. This will depend upon exactly how much you fail to reinvest and how large a gain was in the harmed asset. But not buying property which costs enough can cause at least part of the gain to be taxed.

For example, let us say that you lose a business building to fire. Your insurance company pays you $125,000. Regardless of what you originally paid for the building destroyed, you'll have to buy another which costs at least $125,000. Buying one for less will cause part or all of your gain on the casualty to go to your tax return.

So, the first key to postponing a gain is to reinvest at least as much as the total proceeds you receive, regardless of the original cost or current fair market value of the property you lose.

Buying the Right Type of Property

Besides spending enough, you must also reinvest in the right kind of property. Even if you failed to buy replacement property which cost as much as the total proceeds you received, *part* of the gain might still escape taxes. But, if you do not buy the right type of replacement property, *all* of the gain will be taxed. This will happen even if you spend more than the insurance or other proceeds.

In the example above, you had to spend at least $125,000 on the property replacing what was destroyed. Spending $125,000, or $150,000, or $500,000 on the wrong *type* of property won't keep any gain off the tax return. It will go directly there.

What type of asset should you buy?

Basically, you must purchase one which is the same or similar in service or use as the old one. This means, usually, that if a typewriter is stolen, you should replace it with another typewriter, not a desk or automobile. If a dump truck is wrecked, you will want to invest the insurance proceeds in another dump truck, not a crane or airplane.

The law figures that you had no desire to give up the specific asset that was injured or taken away from you. You must show your honorable motives by reinvesting in property which does basically the same job as the old property.

There is one unusual exception to this rule. When productive business or investment real estate is condemned, most other business or investment real estate can be an acceptable replacement. For example, if the city condemns your factory building because it wants to put a street through it, you can probably replace the building with an apartment complex, an office building, or other business or investment real estate. You can use basically the same rule for replacement you'd have with a tax-free trade (Chapter 18).

This liberal treatment only works with land or buildings which are used for productive business or investment purposes. Your personal residence (nonbusiness, noninvestment property) is handled under other tax rules if it is condemned. The parcels of land a subdivider holds for resale also can't come under this exception because he is planning to sell those items as a department store would stock its own merchandise inventory. But buildings or land you rent to others or use in your own business (rental houses, apartments, shopping centers, warehouses, parking lots, vacant land, office buildings, and others) *do* qualify.

Property which isn't real estate cannot be replaced under this liberal rule. Any type of involuntary conversion (even a condemnation) involving a dump truck, for instance, should result in the owner buying another dump truck. The condemnation of your crane must lead to your purchasing another crane.

And no involuntary conversion other than a condemnation will cause such liberal rules to apply—even to real estate. For example, if a warehouse burns or is destroyed by a storm, it must be replaced by another warehouse. Only if it is condemned can it be replaced by a variety of other types of business or investment real estate.

Time Allowed for Replacement

If you don't buy the replacement asset within the time allowed, all gain on the old property will be recognized—even though you may spend enough and buy the right kind of replacement property. For most situations, the time allowed is more than sufficient, and there is little reason not to meet the deadline.

The replacement period usually starts with the casualty or theft. You have until the end of the first year in which insurance proceeds or other compensation is received, then two more years in which to reinvest. For instance, if your dump truck is wrecked on February 20, 19A, and you receive a check from the insurance company on April 10, 19A, you have from February 20, 19A, to December 31, 19C, to buy another dump truck

Replace Anytime During

2/20/19A to 12/31/19A
19B (the next year)
19C (the final year)

Condemnations of productive business or investment real estate, which get liberal treatment when deciding upon replacement property (above), again are treated favorably. You normally have one additional year in which to replace productive business or investment real estate which is condemned. Instead of meeting a December 31, 19C, deadline, you could probably go as far as December 31, 19D.

Tell the IRS Your Plans

If you intend 1) to reinvest enough, 2) to buy the right type of property, and 3) to meet your deadline, you need to show this in your tax return for the year you would've been taxed on the gain. Then, when you have followed all the rules, you should be free from taxes on the incident.

When you either make your replacement properly or pass the deadline without replacing the old asset, you'll need to notify the IRS, informing them of the state of affairs. If you haven't met one or more of the three rules, you must file an amended tax return for the year of the involuntary conversion which reports the gain as being taxable.

What Inflation Says About Replacement

The type of property to buy and the minimum amount to spend are usually dictated by tax rules. But, since you have a considerable amount of time within which to acquire the replacement property, timing your purchase carefully can help you defend your business against the effects of inflation.

Replacing Equipment

Most items of equipment used in an enterprise decline in value year after year. If a machine is destroyed, but isn't particularly needed at the moment, it may be wise to wait as long as possible before buying another. If you replaced it right away, the new item would merely depreciate without being fully used. On the other hand, the funds from your insurance settlement could be invested at good yields in short-term money market securities until near the end of the time allowed for reinvestment.

If it is needed occasionally before the reinvestment deadline is reached, equipment could be rented from someone else for short periods of time.

As an example, let's assume that equipment is burned, and your insurance proceeds amount to $10,000. Let us also say that the result is a gain, so you will have to reinvest. But you don't often use this particular piece of equipment. Given these circumstances, you will probably want to delay buying replacement property until right before the deadline.

If you have two and one-half years in which to replace it, you can invest the $10,000 at perhaps eight to ten percent interest, yielding in the neighborhood of $2,500 to $3,000, depending on how the interest is compounded. If you buy the equipment right away, and it declines in value across the same period, you might wind up with a $7,000 or $8,000 piece of equipment, instead of $12,500 or $13,000 cash.

A critic might point out that the replacement equipment, as you near the deadline, will cost $12,500 or $13,000. This is certainly true. The other side of the "more expensive equipment" argument, however, is that at the time you buy it, the new asset begins its decline in value from $12,500 or $13,000. If you'd gone the other direction, your machine would now be declining (after more than two years of ownership) from its value of $7,000 or $8,000.

	Delay Reinvestment	Don't Delay Reinvestment
Earnings (Loss) on $10,000 Investment	$ 2,500 to $ 3,000	($2,000) to ($3,000)
Amount You Have at the Reinvestment Deadline	$12,500 to $13,000	$7,000 to $8,000

When a destroyed item is used constantly, this postponement technique won't work. The expense of renting replacement property until the deadline approaches could well offset the gains you'd have from waiting. So, only careful analysis of each individual situation can give the proper course of action.

Replacing Real Estate

In the case of real estate which is harmed by a casualty, it is usually wise to reinvest at the earliest possible moment. Real estate normally increases in value, giving it ideal inflation resistance.

If income-producing property is mortgaged, the return on investment can be much higher than if the same amount is invested in short-term interest-bearing instruments. For example, if you receive a $50,000 insurance settlement from the destruction of your apartment building, you could rebuild or reinvest in another building right away, or you could invest the $50,000 in securities and collect interest until near the reinvestment deadline.

At 10 percent interest, you might receive $10,000 to $15,000 on your $50,000 cash before time to reinvest. On the other hand, assume that the $50,000 is used soon after receipt as a downpayment on a $200,000 building. Assume further that tenants make all payments on the $150,000 mortgage. If it increases in value 10 percent per year, the value of the building would rise by $40,000 or 50,000 during the same time you would have gotten $10,000 or $15,000 by not reinvesting in real estate.

Your $50,000 initial equity in the building would about double with an increase in value of $40,000 or $50,000. On the other hand, $10,000 or $15,000 of interest would increase the $50,000 equity by only about 20 or 30 percent.

	Delay Reinvestment	Don't Delay Reinvestment
Earnings on $50,000	$10,000 to $15,000	$40,000 to $50,000
Amount You Have at the Reinvestment Deadline (including your $50,000)	$60,000 to $65,000	$90,000 to $100,000

Naturally, it takes time to rebuild or to find an acceptable property in which to reinvest. You should neither unduly delay a purchase nor jump at the first deal presented. During the time you're looking for another property, you would be well advised to get a high yield from your insurance proceeds by putting the cash into short-term, interest-paying investments.

Important Points

Few people in business for themselves (whether they have a small clothing store, a pest-control business, or a large manufacturing company) can escape all thefts, casualties, and condemnations. The frequency of such unhappy events seems to be increasing, as shown by more security measures everywhere and crime stories in your daily newspaper.

Depending upon the amount of damage done, and the insurance, court recovery, scrap, or other proceeds you receive, the result can be a gain or loss. A loss is put onto your tax return in the year you experience it.

When the result is a gain, four steps must be taken in order to keep from being taxed. The fact that an involuntary conversion happens because of things beyond your control is irrelevant. What is relevant is whether or not you carefully follow the rules about when and how to replace the property lost. If you fail to properly take any one of these four steps, part or all of your gain will be taxed.

While only part of the gain *may* be taxed if you don't purchase replacement property costing enough, all of the gain *can* be taxed if the amount reinvested is too low. Failure to take any one of the other steps will probably cause your entire gain to be taxed—a tax bill you never anticipated on a gain you didn't want.

Replacement rules are more liberal when you need to reinvest after a condemnation of productive business or investment real estate. But even then, the law must be carefully met in order to postpone taxes.

While waiting for an opportunity to reinvest in either equipment or real estate, you will certainly want to get the highest yield you can from temporary investments. At least this will come close to keeping the purchasing power of your capital the same as it was before the casualty occurred.

Depending upon how much you use equipment, you may be able to better beat inflation by waiting until near the end of the time allowed before buying replacement property. Most equipment declines in value after purchase, which is undesirable if the price of everything else keeps going up.

In the case of almost any conversion of real estate, inflation dictates that you reinvest as soon as possible. Despite predictions of a collapse in prices, real estate has (in most locales) traditionally held its own against inflation. If properly mortgaged, your equity in land or buildings may do better than keep up with inflation.

It may not seem "right" that you could have a tax bill because of a theft or casualty you never wanted. But you can.

All you can do is 1) realize what the possibilities are (both good and bad) and 2) use the rules offered by tax law to save as much in taxes as you can. Uncle Sam wants to help you save taxes. He just wants you to follow his rules.

18

Protecting Capital
with Tax-Free Trades

Sooner or later, you'll need to dispose of a business asset. Equipment may be worn out, too large, too small, or no longer needed. You may own some real estate and want to use your equity in it as a down payment on another property.

If you sell an old asset before buying another, any gain or loss on the sale goes directly to your tax return, sometimes with horrifying consequences. The sale of a worn-out piece of equipment for a good price may result in a large amount of gain being taxed as ordinary income like your salary, rather than as long-term capital gain.

Naturally, these taxes reduce your business capital and personal wealth in a time when inflation is already working to cut your ability to purchase goods and services. Selling an old asset, then buying another one can give assistance to both of these enemies of your business.

People sometimes hear from friends that they can sell a farm or other real estate, then buy a new piece of property without a tax bill. This simply isn't true. These are taxable sales, even if more real estate is purchased. You can postpone a gain from sale only in the case of the sale of your main residence, and then only if you properly reinvest the proceeds in another home.

There is, however, a way to dispose of an asset you no longer want and to use your equity in it to acquire another without that unexpected tax bill. The difference between owing taxes and not owing taxes is in *how* you get rid of your property and acquire someone else's.

Tax-Free Trades—The Ideal Way to Beat Taxes

The best way to postpone taxes when you need to dispose of an asset and acquire another is to use the tax-free trade technique. More effort may be required to arrange a proper exchange than would be expended by selling one asset and buying another, but the tax savings can reward you well.

Actually, the tax-free trade is a fairly flexible method of trading assets. With an involuntary conversion (Chapter 17), you usually need to buy a replacement asset which does virtually the same job as the one destroyed. But under tax-free trade rules, the replacement property can be different.

You could, for example, swap a used typewriter for a calculator, a warehouse for an office building, a shopping center for an apartment complex, a rental house for a duplex, a dump truck for a crane, and so on.

Like selling an old asset for cash and buying another, however, a *taxable* trade causes any gain or loss to go immediately to your tax return. This happens when you swap something you own for another item you want—but one or the other properties isn't the right type.

What is the "Right Type"?

To be a tax-free trade, the item you swap away must be productive business or investment property, and the asset you receive must also be productive business or investment property. We're talking primarily about equipment and real estate which you use in your business or in which you invest—land, buildings, furniture, office equipment, airplanes, vehicles, and others.

Examples of assets which are *not* productive business or investment items are your personal residence, the merchandise inventory you buy for resale, and an automobile not used for business or investment purposes. If you trade away any of these items, or swap productive business or investment property for them, you'll have a tax bill.

Your personal residence may seem to be an "investment," but tax law says that it's used for your personal pleasure—you live in it. A rental house, on the other hand, is productive business property and can be used in a tax-free trade.

Inventory is business property, but it isn't *productive* business property. Productive business property is used over a period of time to conduct your business—not sold to customers at the first opportunity.

The auto you drive to the grocery and use on vacations is not a productive business or investment asset. The car you use in your business is. The first vehicle cannot be involved in a tax-free trade. But the second can.

For example, let's say that you trade merchandise inventory for a typewriter to use in your enterprise, or swap your business truck for a house in which you will live. Both exchanges are taxable because what you're either giving up (inventory) or receiving (personal residence) is not productive business or investment property.

But swapping your business typewriter for a calculator which you will also use in your organization would probably be a tax-free trade. Both are productive business or investment assets.

Incidentally, it does not matter what the property you are giving up or receiving is to the person with whom you are trading. You can swap your old business car to an automobile dealer for a business truck. To the dealer, the truck is inventory (he's taxed); to you, it is a productive business asset. The point is that both what you give up and receive must be productive business or investment property to *you*. It doesn't matter how the other party is taxed.

Personalty for Personalty, Realty for Realty

The exchange must also be personal property for other personal property or real estate for other real estate. The term "personal property," of course, here means business or investment assets which aren't buildings or land. A business automobile, then, is business personal property. If it is traded for a vacant lot (business *real* property), or vice versa, taxes will be due. The vehicle would be better swapped for another business vehicle or piece of business personal property. The vacant lot should be traded for other business or investment real estate.

The fact that a vacant lot is unimproved and an office building is improved real estate is not as important under tax-free trade rules as the fact that they are both business or investment real estate. Such a trade would most likely not be taxed.

Shares of Stock

Something that surprises many people is that shares of stock can't be swapped for other shares of stock in a tax-free trade. Although they are traditionally thought of as investment property, tax law specifically says that shares of stock are not allowed to qualify for an exchange which escapes taxes under these rules.

Don't Postpone Losses

So far, we've just talked about postponing gains with tax-free exchanges. What if it looks like you are going to have a *loss* on disposing of an item? Should you still try to use the tax-free trade technique?

No. If the value of a business or investment asset has declined (and a loss is likely), you'll probably be better off if you sell it than if you trade it. The sale will generate a loss for your tax return which can be used to cut your taxes this year. A tax-free trade will not.

Boot May Cause Problems

The values of items exchanged are often not equal. In these cases, "boot" in the form of cash or other property must be given or received to make up the difference. Boot is anything other than the main subject of the exchange. If you are trading trucks, boot might be cash, shares of stock, a vacant lot, inventory, cattle, etc. When you trade your used truck with a value of $2,000 for a new one worth $9,000, you will have to give $7,000 worth of something extra (boot) to make the deal even.

If you are swapping pieces of business or investment real estate, boot is cash, shares of stock, your private residence, inventory, cattle, a mobile home, or anything else which isn't business or investment real estate.

For example, assume that you trade your four-unit apartment building worth $100,000 for someone's duplex worth $60,000. He must give you cash, an expensive automobile, shares of stock, or something else to make sure that you receive a total of $100,000.

The presence of boot in an exchange may cause you to owe some taxes, especially if you receive the boot or if you give boot other than cash.

Giving Boot

When you give boot, tax law figures that you are really just selling the boot. Let's say that you trade your $2,000 car for an $8,000 truck and give $6,000 worth of blue-chip stock as boot. If the stock cost you $4,000, you have a $2,000 taxable gain ($6,000 value, less $4,000 cost). If you paid $10,000 for the stock, you have a $4,000 loss for your tax return ($6,000 value, less $10,000 cost). But if you give $6,000 cash, you'd have no gain or loss. Why? The cost and value of cash are the same.

	Stock	Stock	Cash
Value of Boot You Give	$6,000	$ 6,000	$6,000
Cost or Other Basis of the Boot	4,000	10,000	6,000
Your Taxable Gain (Loss)	$2,000	($ 4,000)	$ -0-

When you must give boot in an exchange, consider trying to get the other party to take an asset in which you have a loss. Besides not having any taxes on the exchange itself, you might be able to generate a tax-saving loss.

The next best alternative is to give cash. Although it may be a scarce resource these days, the IRS judges cash to cost the same as its fair market value. The result? No gain or loss comes from using it as boot.

Boot in which you have a gain should be given only when you can't avoid it. The deal could generate a tax bill without producing any cash with which to pay it.

Receiving Boot

When you receive boot, you can have a taxable gain, but not a loss. This gain is the smaller of 1) the boot or 2) the gain you'd have if you sold your property outright (instead of trading it).

Assume that you exchange your $100,000 apartment building for a $60,000 duplex. The other party has to give you $40,000 in cash or other boot to make the deal even. If you would have a $60,000 gain from an outright sale of the building for $100,000, the gain you show on your tax return is only $40,000 (the amount of the boot). See Case 1 below.

If you would have a $30,000 gain from selling the building, $30,000 (the entire gain) goes to your tax return, since it is the smaller number. See Case 2 below.

		Case 1	Case 2
Total of What You're Receiving:			
	Duplex	$ 60,000	$ 60,000
	Boot	(A) 40,000	(A) 40,000
		$100,000	$100,000
Basis of What You're Giving Up (Your Apartment Building)		40,000	70,000
Gain You'd Have if You Sold Your Apartment Building Outright for $100,000 Cash		(B) $ 60,000	(B) $ 30,000
Your Taxable Gain (Smaller of A or B)		$ 40,000	$ 30,000

Think twice before you accept a considerable amount of boot in an exchange. In some cases, the result may be the same as selling your property for cash (Case 2 above). You might be much better off trading your property for something closer in value. Let's take the two cases above and trade your apartment building for real estate of equal value.

	Case 1	Case 2
Total of What You're Receiving:		
Duplex	$100,000	$100,000
Boot	(A)____-0-____	(A)____-0-____
	$100,000	$100,000
Basis of What You're Giving Up		
(Your Apartment Building)	40,000	70,000
Gain You'd Have if You Sold Your Apartment Building Outright for $100,000 Cash	(B) $ 60,000	(B) $ 30,000
Your Taxable Gain (Smaller of A or B)	$ -0-	$ -0-

By taking a more valuable property in trade (and avoiding the receipt of boot), you've managed to keep a gain off your tax return. Just being choosy in what you'll accept in trade can save you thousands of dollars in taxes.

Offsetting Mortgages and Other Boot

One technicality that can trick you in a basically tax-free exchange is that any mortgage on property you trade away is treated as cash boot received by you. So, if you swap your warehouse (which has a $50,000 mortgage on it) for someone's office building, the $50,000 mortgage you give away is "boot" received by you.

Fortunately, tax law allows a certain amount of offsetting of boot. If the office building you're taking in exchange for your warehouse also has a mortgage on it, your $50,000 boot may be reduced or completely eliminated. You just offset the mortgage on the property you are receiving against the mortgage on the property you give up.

It's a good idea to get your tax advisor involved at an early stage on trades other than simple equipment swaps. He may be able to save you considerable taxes—especially if you are both giving and receiving boot.

An Additional Incentive

Many people just aren't concerned about the need to postpone a gain on the sale of business assets. They do not figure that much gain will result. And they believe that any gain which does arise will be taxed as a long-term capital gain.

Aside from the fact that a capital gain is also taxed—less severely than ordinary income such as salary or interest, but still taxed—this gain may not be a capital gain at all. The sale of assets which have been depreciated often leads to part or all of the gain being fully taxed as unprotected ordinary income.

Congress sees owners of buildings and equipment depreciating their assets rapidly to get deductions. These deductions offset sales, interest, commissions, and other types of income which would be fully taxable if they reached the tax return. So, tax rules say that when you sell these depreciated assets, part or all of the gain on them will be taxed as though it were the income you covered with depreciation deductions.

If you buy a truck for $10,000 and depreciate it down to $3,000, then sell it for $10,000, you have $7,000 of gain. This gain is taxable like sales, interest, or other unprotected income. If you sell the truck for $12,000, you have the same $7,000 of ordinary income. Only the remaining $2,000 of gain will be taxed as a capital gain ($12,000 sales price, less $10,000 original cost). The government figures that you used the $7,000 of depreciation to cut taxes on sales, interest, and similar income. Now that you are selling the truck, any gain up to the original cost will be turned into the same type of income that the depreciation sheltered.

A sale of real estate which has been depreciated will not always give as severe a result as you'd have for the truck. But no guarantees can be given that all gain will be long-term capital gain.

So, a gain from selling—instead of trading—business property may not be treated as leniently as you might think. You could have an enormous tax bill. Part of the cash you are counting on to buy new assets for your business could be taken away by taxes.

Important Points

Eventually, every business needs to replace an asset with another. The property may be as small as a worn-out typewriter or as complex as an apartment building from which all the tax shelter potential has been drained.

Your choice is one of having the disposal of the item completely taxed (perhaps severely) or possibly not taxed at all. When the item is of small value and the resulting tax is minor, convenience may dictate a taxable sale, then the purchase of another asset with cash. If the potential tax bill is large, however, the price of convenience is high. When you work hard to build your business, you will want to work just as hard to preserve your capital.

Both what you trade away and what you receive must be productive business or investment property. If assets which are anything else to you (such as your private residence, shares of stock, or inventory) enter the transaction, you'll probably have a tax bill.

And be sure that you're trading personal property for personal property or real estate for real estate. Mixing the two general types of assets would cause the exchange to be completely taxable.

As you steer your business through what can sometimes be an uncertain environment, you should take advantage of every break available to you—especially tax breaks. The tax-free trade is one way in which you can use tax rules to your benefit. The savings in taxes can be enormous.

19

Taking Maximum Advantage of Capital Gains and Losses

As you saw in Chapters 17 and 18, it's best to avoid taxes completely when you dispose of assets. The less tax you pay, the more cash you have with which to make additional money. You should use a tax-free trade or involuntary conversion whenever possible. But sometimes it just isn't possible to avoid a taxable gain.

If you are caught in this situation, one surprisingly straightforward way to save taxes is to take advantage of another set of rules that Congress intentionally put into tax law for the business owner and investor. These are the laws on capital gains and losses.

Taking advantage of favorable treatment of capital gains and losses is much more involved, however, than just selling an asset and calling the gain a capital gain. The timing of sales of different assets can often result in a much lower tax bill than if you sell items randomly. Mixing different types of gains and losses from sales in the same year will determine whether some are taxed lightly, whether you lose their usefulness, or whether you wind up with the worst of all cases—a long-term capital loss carryover.

What Is a Capital Asset?

To have a capital gain or loss, you must usually have a capital asset. The sale of certain other types of property can sometimes give a gain or loss which may become a capital gain or loss, but this is not automatic. Since capital gains and losses can be used to such advantage, tax law is careful about what may be called a capital asset.

Inventory, accounts and notes receivable, depreciable business property, and a few other items are not capital assets.

So, if you own a supermarket, your groceries (inventory) are not capital assets. When you sell them, the result is not a capital gain or loss. If you sell merchandise on credit, your receivables from customers are not capital assets.

Most people think that depreciable business assets such as equipment and buildings are capital assets. They are not. However, part of the gain from the sale of such property (particularly buildings) *may* turn into long-term capital gain.

If these things aren't capital assets, then what types of assets are?

Usually, investments you make in land, gold, shares of stock, or other items which you do not depreciate are capital assets. Even certain nonbusiness items are included. Your private residence, lake lot, nonbusiness automobile, and sailboat are all capital assets. (You don't depreciate them and they are not inventory of your business.)

Individual or Corporation?

An individual who has a capital gain or loss is taxed differently than is a corporation. This chapter shows how to save taxes if you have capital gains and losses as an individual or as a partner in a partnership. Chapter 20 explains how your corporation can keep its taxes low with capital gains and losses.

The Holding Period Makes the Difference

Let's say you sell something that you know for certain is a capital asset. Do you now have a long-term capital gain?

Not necessarily.

The length of time you own a capital asset determines whether any gain or loss is short-term or long-term. When you buy an item, the holding period usually starts the day after its purchase, and includes the day you sell it. You count by months, not days.

For example, if you bought an asset on January 15, 19A, the first day counted for your holding period is January 16, 19A. To have a long-term capital gain or loss, you must own the item for at least 12 months and one day. This means that you could sell it on January 16, 19B. January 16, 19A, through January 15, 19B, is exactly one year. Since you need at least one extra day, counting January 16, 19B, should meet the requirement.

Short-Term Capital Gain

When you sell a capital asset that you've not owned for at least one year and a day, you will have a short-term capital gain or loss. If you do not have other sales of capital assets during the year, a short-term capital gain becomes unprotected ordinary income. It is taxed like salary, sales, or commissions. If you're in the 35 percent tax bracket and take a $10,000 short-term capital gain, your taxes could amount to $3,500 (35 percent of $10,000).

Long-Term Capital Gain

When you sell a capital asset which you have owned for more than one year, the result is a long-term capital gain or loss. By itself, a long-term capital gain is taxed leniently. Out of the entire gain, only 40 percent is actually taxed. The other 60 percent escapes taxes.

Assume, for instance, that you have a $10,000 long-term capital gain. Of the total, 60 percent escapes. The other 40 percent ($4,000) is all that's taxed. This shows dramatically the difference that foresight can make. If you had sold the item before the one-year-and-one-day holding period was up, the entire $10,000 would have been taxed. By keeping the item just a little longer, the taxable gain can be reduced to only $4,000. If you are in the common 35 percent tax bracket, one day could make a difference of over $2,000 in your tax bill.

	Short-Term Capital Gain	Long-Term Capital Gain
Capital Gain	$10,000	$10,000
Less: Long-Term Capital Gain Deduction (60% × Gain)	-0-	6,000
Amount Subject to Tax	$10,000	$ 4,000
Your Tax Rate	× .35	× .35
Your Tax on the Gain	$ 3,500	$ 1,400

Short-Term Capital Loss

When you sell a capital asset you've not owned for at least one year and a day, and the result is a loss, you have a short-term capital loss. If you have no other sales of capital assets during the year, a short-term capital loss can offset up to $3,000 of your ordinary unprotected income.

For example, a $3,000 short-term capital loss can knock $3,000 off your income from other sources, such as profits, salary, interest, or commissions. If it is only $2,000, the loss can offset $2,000 of such income.

But your annual limit is $3,000. A $10,000 short-term capital loss can reduce income this year by only $3,000. The remaining $7,000 ($10,000 less $3,000) is carried over to be offset against your income in later years.

Long-Term Capital Loss

A capital asset you hold for at least 12 months and a day, then sell at a loss, will give you a long-term capital loss. Since a long-term capital gain is treated favorably, a long-term capital loss is treated *un*favorably. Every two dollars of such loss can reduce only one dollar of unprotected ordinary income. And your annual limit is again $3,000.

For example, a $2,000 long-term capital loss will offset $1,000 of income such as profits, salary, interest, or commissions. A $6,000 long-term capital loss will cover one-half of $6,000, or $3,000, of ordinary income.

A $10,000 long-term capital loss will still only do away with $3,000 of ordinary income in any one year. And it takes $6,000 of long-term capital loss to do the job at 50 cents against the dollar. This means that $6,000 of the $10,000 is used to reach your annual limit of $3,000. So, $4,000 ($10,000 less $6,000) is carried over to reduce your income in later years.

	Using Short-Term Capital Loss	Using Long-Term Capital Loss
Ordinary Income	$10,000	$10,000
Reduction You Can Get This Year with a $10,000 Capital Loss	3,000	3,000
Ordinary Income Remaining to be Taxed	$ 7,000	$ 7,000
Loss Carried Over to Use in Later Years:		
Short-Term ($10,000 − $3,000)	$ 7,000	
Long-Term ($10,000 − $6,000)		$ 4,000

As you see, a long-term capital loss, by itself, is the least desirable of the four situations: short-term capital gain, long-term capital gain, short-term capital loss, or long-term capital loss. It can be used only on a two-for-one basis against ordinary income. The other half is lost.

Mixing Capital Gains and Losses

Although long- and short-term capital losses have a limited use for reducing ordinary income, both types can be used as a dollar-for-dollar offset against capital gains—without an annual limit. A $3,000 short-term capital loss can reduce your regular income from other sources by as much as $3,000. A $20,000 capital loss will still only offset $3,000 of such income in any one year, leaving $17,000 to be carried over.

But your short-term capital loss can fully offset the same amount of short- or long-term capital gains. If you apply this $20,000 loss against a $20,000 capital gain, the result is a $-0- remaining gain.

	Ordinary Income	Capital Gain
Your Income or Gain	$20,000	$20,000
Reduction You Can Get This Year with a $20,000 Short-Term Capital Loss	3,000	20,000
Remainder (to be Taxed)	$17,000	$ -0-
Short-Term Capital Loss to be Carried Over ($20,000 − $ 3,000 used) ($20,000 − $20,000 used)	$17,000	$ -0-

It takes a $6,000 long-term capital loss to reduce your ordinary income by $3,000. But such loss is good dollar for dollar against capital gains. So, a $6,000 long-term capital loss could offset $6,000 of short-term or long-term capital gain.

Likewise, the long-term capital loss doesn't run into the $3,000 annual limit when you use it against capital gains. A $20,000 long-term capital loss would offset $3,000 of regular income and leave a $14,000 carryover ($20,000 loss, less the $6,000 it takes to offset $3,000 of ordinary income). This same $20,000 capital loss could offset $20,000 of capital gain, with no carryover required.

	Ordinary Income	Capital Gain
Your Income or Gain	$20,000	$20,000
Reduction You Can Get This Year with a $20,000 Long-Term Capital Loss	3,000	20,000
Remainder (to be Taxed)	$17,000	$ -0-
Long-Term Capital Loss to be Carried Over		
($20,000 − $ 6,000 used)	$14,000	
($20,000 − $20,000 used)		$ -0-

Timing Your Gains and Losses for Lower Taxes

Since capital losses, especially long-term capital losses, do so poorly against ordinary income, it seems a shame to let them go to your tax return alone. The same idea applies to short-term capital gains, which are fully taxable if they reach your return by themselves.

The only item you might like to have appear on your tax return by itself is a long-term capital gain. It will get favorable treatment.

If you own a variety of assets, you have some control over what is placed on your tax return each year. Many people, to their detriment, do not take advantage of this tax-reducing fact. But all that is required is to keep in mind, as you go through the year, how capital gains and losses can intermix. Near the end of the year, you'll want to take a close look at your overall tax situation and make any additional sales of capital assets needed to properly use the gains or losses you already have.

For example, assume that you take a $5,000 short-term capital gain in one year and a $5,000 long-term capital loss in the next. If you are in the 40 percent tax bracket, you give up $2,000 of cash as taxes on the $5,000 gain. The next year, your $5,000 long-term capital loss offsets only $2,500 of ordinary income (50 cents against the dollar). Your long-term capital loss saves you 40 percent of this $2,500, or $1,000 in taxes.

Year 1

Short-Term Capital Gain	$5,000
Your Tax Rate	× .40
Your Tax	$2,000

Year 2

Long-Term Capital Loss	$5,000
Portion Lost When Offset Against	
Ordinary Income	× .50
Usable Against Ordinary Income	$2,500
Your Tax Rate	× .40
Your Tax Savings	$1,000

What would happen if you saw the short-term capital gain approaching your tax return alone and deliberately took the capital loss in the same year?

Your loss would completely offset the gain, on a dollar-for-dollar basis, leaving no gain or loss. Although you wouldn't save $1,000 of taxes in the second year, you would not pay an extra $2,000 in the first year. So, you would save a total of about $1,000 through tax planning.

Year 1

Short-Term Capital Gain	$5,000
Less: Long-Term Capital Loss	(5,000)
Amount Subject to Tax	$ -0-

If you take a long-term capital gain this year, do you want to take losses to offset it now, or should you sell assets on which you have losses in later years?

Assume that the $5,000 gain above was a long-term capital gain. Only 40 percent of such gain, or $2,000, would be taxed to you if it went to your return alone. The other 60 percent of the gain is discarded. If your tax rate is also 40 percent, your taxes on the $2,000 remaining gain would be $800.

Long-Term Capital Gain	$5,000
	× .40
Portion of Gain to be Taxed	$2,000
Your Tax Rate	× .40
Your Tax	$ 800

You saw earlier that a $5,000 long-term capital loss could save you $1,000 of taxes if you were in the 40 percent tax bracket. A short-term capital loss could save you even more. But, if you use either one to offset $5,000 of long-term capital gain, they'll only save you $800—because that is all the taxes you will owe on such a gain.

So, you'd be better off to allow the long-term capital gain to go to your tax return alone this year, and take your capital losses next year—providing you are in the 40 percent tax bracket.

Of course, taking maximum advantage of capital gains and losses means regularly doing tax planning for your *own* individual situation. If you are in a different tax bracket, or if you have much larger capital losses, you may find it helpful to offset any capital gain or capital loss you take during a year.

The best solution for many people seems to be to let their long-term capital gains reach the tax return by themselves but not to permit either short-term capital gains or long-term capital losses to get there alone.

Unlocking Those "Locked-In" Gains

You'll occasionally buy property for investment and observe it rapidly go up in value in less than a year. Then you will want your cash out of it to enter another venture. Since you have not held the asset for at least 12 months and a day, the entire gain would be short-term (fully taxable at high rates). Yet the new project looks attractive.

What can you do? Are you locked into the original investment until it goes beyond the one-year mark?

People who are in this position often have accumulated, over a period of years, other investments—shares of stock, gold, and other capital assets—which have declined in value below their purchase prices. It is human nature to want to keep these "dogs" until they eventually turn around and can be sold at gains. But by selling these bad investments now, you may be able to get your cash out of that winning investment virtually tax-free.

Let's say, for example, that you have a $25,000 short-term capital gain in land and you want to sell it so that you can use the cash for other projects. But you are in the 40 percent tax bracket. Selling now would cost you $10,000 in taxes (40 percent of $25,000).

If you have $25,000 of long- or short-term capital losses in other investments (shares of stock, precious metals, real estate, or other capital assets), you can offset your gain by selling these losing investments in the same year. Although you don't wait for the poor investments to turn around and show gains, you *do* save $10,000 in taxes. In a sense, then, your "dogs" gain $10,000 in value overnight. They unlock the cash in your good investment through effective tax planning.

	Not Using Your Losses	Using Your Losses
Short-Term Capital Gain	$25,000	$25,000
Capital Losses	-0-	25,000
Amount Which Is Taxable	$25,000	$ -0-
Your Tax Rate	× .40	× .40
Your Taxes	$10,000	$ -0-

Consider a "Small Business Corporation"

When you're starting a corporation or turning your existing business into a corporation, it is an unpleasant time to talk about the possibility of selling your stock at a loss. But let us stop for a moment to look at what would happen if you tired of the business or wanted your cash out of it for another venture, and wound up taking a loss on your investment.

Shares of stock in your corporation would be a capital asset. Selling these shares at a loss would cause a capital loss. If you sell them after owning them for more than a year, you would have a long-term capital loss.

After reading how badly capital losses are treated, you can see what a problem you might have. Let's say you sold the corporation for a $100,000 loss. Unless you had capital gains against which to offset it, the use of this loss would be limited.

If you'd owned the stock for no more than a year, you could deduct a $3,000 loss each year for the next 33 years and $1,000 of loss in the 34th year. Sounds pretty bad, doesn't it? But the situation would be worse if you had owned the corporation for longer than a year.

Half of a long-term capital loss is disregarded if it must be offset against profits, salary, or other ordinary income. Of a $100,000 loss, you would throw away $50,000. Then you could deduct a $3,000 loss each year for the next 16 years and $2,000 in the 17th year.

Isn't there a better way?

Yes. With a "Small Business Corporation," you could deduct the whole $100,000 in the year you sell your stock at a loss. Being able to deduct the entire loss right away might completely eliminate your income taxes for several years.

How does this work?

Your corporation must be a "small business corporation." This means, roughly, that the stock issued can't go over $1,000,000 and less than half the corporation's gross receipts can come from passive sources such as interest, rent, dividends, royalties, and gains on the sale of shares of stock. And only the person to whom the stock is originally issued by the corporation qualifies for this special deal.

The best time to talk to your tax advisor about these requirements is when you start a corporation or incorporate a going business.

If your corporation qualifies, you can deduct up to a $100,000 loss ($50,000 if you are not "married, filing jointly") in the year you sell your stock. When the loss is over $100,000 (or $50,000), the excess is a capital loss.

If you don't have enough income to soak up all that loss, it can be carried over and used to offset income in other years.

Let's stop looking at possible misfortune and see what would happen if your corporation prospered. You might think that you would sacrifice something here in order to get favorable treatment if the business went bad. But you do not. Selling your shares of stock at a gain would result in a capital gain. If you'd owned the stock for more than a year, it would be a long-term capital gain; if not, a short-term capital gain.

Important Points

Almost everyone owns capital assets of one type or another. Gains on all such items are taxable. Unfortunately, however, losses on nonbusiness, noninvestment assets (such as your private residence or nonbusiness auto) are not deductible unless the loss is caused by a theft or casualty.

The length of time you've owned a capital asset determines whether a gain or loss for its sale is a long- or short-term capital gain or loss. If you have held property for at least one year and a day, the gain or loss is long-term; if not, it is short-term.

Long-term capital gains receive lenient treatment if they go through your tax return without other capital gains or losses. But long-term capital losses are treated badly. If you know that you're going to take a loss on the sale of a capital asset, it is better to sell it before you have owned it for more than a year. At least you will have a short-term capital loss which can be used dollar-for-dollar (up to $3,000) against ordinary income.

When you know that you'll show a gain on the sale of a capital asset, it is better to wait until you have a long-term capital gain than to take a short-term capital gain currently. When it isn't possible to wait until the short-term capital gain turns into a long-term gain, however, you will want to take enough capital losses on sales of other investments to soak up the gain. In this way, you unlock the gain in your winning investment without much tax effect.

Try to avoid having short-term capital gains, short-term capital losses over $3,000, or any long-term capital losses reach your tax return alone. Short-term capital gains are taxed as if they are unprotected profits, salary, or similar income. You can't get any use out of a short-term capital loss above $3,000 without carrying it over to another year.

And half of a long-term capital loss is wasted when it is used to offset ordinary income. Two dollars of loss are required to reduce one dollar of income. As with short-term capital losses, no more than $3,000 of ordinary income (using up $6,000 of long-term capital loss) can be offset per year.

By planning ahead, you can take advantage of one of the easiest ways of manipulating your tax bill. All you have to do is watch your holding periods and be careful about the combination of gains and losses going into your tax return each year. Rules for capital gains and losses seem tailor-made for the business owner or investor. You should take maximum advantage of them in your effort to protect your business from the tax collector.

20

Capital Gains and Losses for Your Corporation

As you saw in Chapter 19, you can only have a capital gain or loss if you sell a capital asset—anything except inventory, business receivables, depreciable business property, and a few other items.

And a capital asset sold after you own it for at least 12 months and one day gives a long-term capital gain or loss. Selling a capital asset you've owned for less time results in a short-term capital gain or loss.

Chapter 19 gave methods for saving taxes if you found capital gains and losses going to your individual income tax return. This chapter explains the same approach for a corporation.

You'll See Some Differences

Although a corporation can offset its long- and short-term capital gains and losses against each other like an individual does on his tax return, there are two big differences:

1) A corporation is taxed differently on its long-term capital gains, and

2) A corporation can't use its capital losses to cut ordinary income from other sources, such as its profits.

Short-Term Capital Gain

If a corporation has no other sales of capital assets or casualties during the year, a short-term capital gain becomes ordinary income and is taxed like interest or profits.

Long-Term Capital Gain

An individual can throw away 60 percent of a long-term capital gain which reaches his tax return alone. He's taxed only on the remaining 40 percent.

But a corporation is taxed on the whole gain. It can add the entire gain to all its other income. Or, it can figure the tax separately on its long-term capital gains at 28 percent and add the result to the tax on its other income. The choice you make will depend on the tax bracket your corporation is in.

Let's say your corporation has a low-income year. It is in the 15 percent tax bracket. A $10,000 long-term capital gain reaches your corporate tax return alone. Which option should you take?

You have a choice of letting the capital gain be taxed with your corporation's other income at 15 percent ($1,500 of taxes on a $10,000 gain). Or you can have the gain taxed at the alternative rate of 28 percent ($2,800 of taxes on a $10,000 gain). The choice is obvious.

What if you have a good year? Let us say that your corporation has the same $10,000 of long-term capital gain when it's in the 40 percent tax bracket. In this situation, letting the gain be combined with your other income would subject it to the 40 percent rate ($4,000 of taxes on a $10,000 gain). So, your proper choice would be the alternative 28 percent tax ($2,800 of taxes).

Short-Term Capital Loss

An individual who does not have any capital gain against which to offset a short-term capital loss can use it in another way. He can wipe out up to $3,000 of his salary, profits, or other ordinary income with it each year until it is used up.

A corporation cannot. Any short-term capital loss which isn't "soaked up" by capital gains is carried back three years and forward five years. It is used in those other years to offset capital gains. If a short-term capital loss is taken back to earlier years, your corporation may get a refund of taxes already paid. When carried forward, the loss saves taxes in later years by cutting capital gains.

Assume, for example, that your corporation has a $4,000 capital gain and a $10,000 short-term capital loss during the same year. When you offset the two against each other, the result is a $6,000 short-term capital loss ($10,000 short-term capital loss, less your $4,000 capital gain). If you had capital gains in any of the last three years, the $6,000 remaining loss is now offset against them. If the capital gains of the last three years don't use up this $6,000, it is carried forward to be offset against capital gains you may have during the next five years.

Long-Term Capital Loss

Like a short-term capital loss, an individual can use a long-term capital loss on his tax return to cut his ordinary income.

But a corporation must again carry the loss back three years and forward five to use against capital gains. Oddly, a long-term capital loss turns into a short-term capital loss when your corporation carries it back or forward. This means that the loss will be offset first against short-term capital gains, then against long-term capital gains.

The example of the short-term capital loss above would differ little if the loss had been a long-term capital loss. As it was carried back or over, the $6,000 long-term capital loss would have changed into a short-term capital loss to be used first against short-term capital gains, then against long-term capital gains.

Keep On Mixing

Before they go to your corporation's tax return alone, of course, all capital gains and losses are offset against each other. Even capital loss carrybacks and carryovers are mixed with them.

Both long- and short-term capital losses can be offset dollar-for-dollar, without limit, against capital gains. For example, a $50,000 capital loss would cut a $70,000 long- or short-term capital gain down to $20,000 ($70,000 less $50,000).

This is extremely important to your corporation as it goes through a period of years with occasional sales of capital assets. Something as simple as careful timing of these sales may help greatly in the job of minimizing your corporation's taxes.

Why Careful Timing Is More Critical Now

At the worst, an individual can use a capital loss to cut his income from other sources—profits, interest, commissions, and others. Because it can't, a corporation might not get any use at all out of a capital loss. Or, the use might be postponed for several years.

Assume, for instance, that your corporation takes a large capital loss in year 19D. Let's say that it did not have any capital gains in the three earlier years (19A, 19B, and 19C), so you cannot apply for a refund. And, as (bad) luck would have it, your corporation doesn't have a capital gain for another five years (until 19I). Your capital loss carryover can only be used in that fifth year.

19A	No Capital Gains
19B	No Capital Gains
19C	No Capital Gains
19D	Large Capital Loss
19E	No Capital Gains
19F	No Capital Gains
19G	No Capital Gains
19H	No Capital Gains
19I	Capital Gain

If it owns a variety of assets, your corporation has some control over what goes to its tax return each year. If it has a capital loss, your corporation can sell another asset in order to use the loss. Preferably, the corporation will sell something in which it has a short-term capital gain. (*Long*-term capital gains which reach the tax return alone may receive preferential treatment.)

On the other hand, if it sees a short-term capital *gain* (taxed as ordinary income) going to the tax return alone, your corporation can sell capital assets in which it has losses. Either short- or long-term capital losses can be used to eliminate capital gains dollar-for-dollar.

For example, let's say that you are a couple of weeks away from the end of your corporation's tax year end. You notice $15,000 of short-term capital gain for the year—but no other capital transactions. Remember? That was the sale of shares of stock back in March when you needed the cash. Now it is going to cost you some taxes.

Or is it? You can now sell some other capital asset that's gone down about $15,000. You may have to sell more than one to come up to that figure, but be careful to not take more capital losses than the $15,000. You'll wind up with a loss carryback or carryforward. All you want to do is to wipe out the $15,000 short-term capital loss—not generate a capital loss carryback or carryover which you may not be able to use for several years.

Important Points

Many corporations, sooner or later, own capital assets. Most gains and losses on the sales of these capital assets are not treated as favorably as they would be for an individual. A long-term capital gain is likely to be hit harder, and capital losses can't be used to offset income from sources such as business profits or interest income.

But, a corporation's long-term capital gain may actually be taxed at a lower rate than it could be for the stockholders of the corporation. A low-income corporation might see its long-term capital gains taxed at 15 percent. Even with the favorable tax treatment allowed an individual, he might be taxed at a considerably higher rate on his own return.

Although it must offset its capital losses only against capital gains, a corporation doesn't have to worry (as an individual does) about half of its long-term capital losses being wasted (Chapter 19). A corporation's capital losses are offset dollar-for-dollar against capital gains.

Near the end of each year, it is important to determine what capital gains and losses your corporation has for the year—and what capital loss carryovers it has. If you find unused capital losses, you may be able to turn a considerable amount of other capital assets into cash tax-free. Just sell enough of these assets so that the gains on them equal the losses you already have.

When you have capital gains (especially short-term capital gains) headed for the tax return alone, consider selling some capital assets in which you have losses. This would let your corporation stop the taxes on those gains before the tax return knows they're coming.

Whether you are doing business as an individual or as a corporation, tax breaks such as the special treatment granted to capital gains and losses are yours to use. Be sure to take full advantage of the tax-saving devices which Uncle Sam freely offers.

21

Installment Sales Can Cut Taxes Three Ways

Many businesses regularly sell products for which the buyer can't pay cash. These are usually large items such as cars, homes, appliances, and musical instruments, but may include clothing and others. The customer can either get a loan through a bank or lending company, or the business itself can provide the financing.

Is there any difference in your income taxes between letting the bank lend to your customers and providing the loans yourself?

Yes, there is a great deal of difference. If a bank provides financing, the entire sale is taxable to you at the time it is made. Of course, many people want nothing to do with loaning money to their customers and accept this tax burden. They hope to find relief in other tax breaks. And there's certainly no shortage of tax savings elsewhere.

But, other individuals are able to regularly finance their own sales. As a result, they are taxed as they collect the payments, rather than at the time of the actual sale. For them, taxes are postponed.

Aside from regular sales, an enterprise will occasionally need to sell a piece of equipment, such as a car, crane, or lathe. As you saw in Chapter 18, the tax-free trade is a much better technique for disposing of unneeded equipment and buildings than is an outright sale, but sometimes such a swap can't be arranged. Rather than have all taxes due at the time of the sale, the installment sale method can be used to make part of the taxes due as each payment is received from the buyer.

An enormous tax bill can result from the sale of real estate, such as a building which has been depreciated over a long period of time. The installment sale technique can be used for a sale of real estate either by a person who regularly sells such property or by an individual who rarely does so. It does not matter whether the real estate has been used for business purposes or for personal enjoyment. It can postpone taxes for both.

So, the installment method can be used in three situations:

1) Regular sales of inventory,

2) Occasional sales of equipment and other personal property, and

3) Any sale of real estate.

Regular Sales of Inventory

When your business is selling products for which your customers are unable to pay cash, someone has to provide the financing. In some businesses, such as automobile sales, it is customary for a bank, finance company, or credit company associated with the dealer to lend the money. In other businesses, such as appliances or furniture, there is not such a clearly-defined custom. The funds may be lent by a bank or by the seller.

If the seller provides the financing on a regular basis, these sales may qualify for the installment sales method. This means, of course, that sales aren't taxed when they are made, but over the period in which cash is collected.

For example, let's say that you sell an item for $500 and require $50 as a down payment. Then you receive another $50 in payments for the year of the sale and $100 each year for the next four years. If the item you sold for $500 cost you $300, this means that you have a $200 gross profit on the entire deal ($500 price, less $300 cost). The gross profit rate for the deal is 40 percent ($200 gross profit, divided by a $500 price). To this point, the transaction would look as follows:

A)	Sales Price	$500
	Cost of Item	300
B)	Your Gross Profit	$200
	Gross Profit Rate (B divided by A)	40%

So, 40 percent of each payment is gross profit to be reported on your tax return. If $100 is received each year, as assumed above, 40 percent, or $40, of each year's payments are taxable gross profit. This contrasts with being taxed on the entire $200 gross profit in the year of the sale if the installment method is not used.

	Installment Method	Regular Method
Sales	$500	$500
Collections	$100	$500
× Gross Profit Rate	× 40%	× 40%
Taxable Profit This Year	$ 40	$200

The numbers used in this example may not be large enough to make the installment method sound advantageous. You only put $160 less profit on your tax return for the year. But, when you substitute an entire enterprise's regular sales for the figures used, the tax postponement possibilities can be outstanding.

Borrowing on Receivables

The point at which many people balk at doing their own financing is when they realize that doing it might soak up additional capital in a business which is already strapped for cash. You say that you barely have enough capital to buy and carry inventory, let alone continue to carry the inventory while a customer uses it?

The answer to this objection is that banks and other financial institutions lend money on good receivables. If you have the buyer put down a reasonable down payment and fill out a credit form, lending institutions will often loan you at least part of the face amount of the note receivable. The down payment you receive from your customer can help fill the gap in capital caused by carrying inventory after it leaves your business.

The bank with which you currently work may not lend on receivables. Frequently, smaller banks are unable to justify hiring people who have expertise in different types of business lending. And larger banks sometimes lose sight of the small business, making loans only to medium and large enterprises.

Shopping for bank services is like shopping for any other item you need for your company. You have to keep looking until you find the exact product or service which suits you. If your banker gladly finances automobiles, but gets high blood pressure when you mention a business loan, you may need a different bank.

Higher Prices

Few banks will lend anywhere near 100 percent of the face amount of the notes you take to them. Does this mean that you'll have difficulty buying inventory to replace that which was sold?

People who buy from a business which finances its own sales often expect to pay more than they would be charged elsewhere for the same items. The convenience of not having to go to a lending institution for a loan is usually worth the extra price. In fact, many people are not as concerned about the price of a product as they are about how much the payments are. In a period of inflation, this can be a valuable way for you to increase prices at least as fast as the rate of inflation without losing sales.

So, with higher prices, you may be able to buy new inventory without the difficulty you imagine. Some cash will come in with the customer's down payment. With a higher sales price than normal, the bank may well be able to lend enough to purchase additional inventory. Even though the lender will not advance you the entire face of each note, the combination of down payments and installment notes may far exceed the cost of replacement inventory.

Interest Rates

A third objection to a business providing its own financing is that banks charge what seem to be exhorbitant interest rates for business loans from time to time. If you mortgage your receivables, will you be able to make the payments when interest is high?

Consumers are used to paying even higher rates of interest when a business provides its own financing than if they have to qualify for a loan at a bank. So, if the bank is charging 14 percent, customers will probably not object too strongly if a business charges 18 percent. Again, many customers are more concerned about whether or not they can handle the monthly payments than they are about the interest rate.

When you are constantly in touch with banks, you will almost always know approximately what they will charge. Your rate to customers can vary accordingly, so you should be able to keep the interest rates you charge higher than those you pay. Your higher rate to customers can result in a welcome addition to the normal profit you make from sales.

Another advantage of staying in contact with your representative at the bank is that you'll have a general idea of what portion of each customer note the lender will return to you in loans. If the bank will soon be lending a lesser portion of the face amount of each note because of tighter money, you can either raise your prices on merchandise or demand a larger down payment on each sale you finance. Either action or both can help you keep enough cash flow to meet your needs.

Collections

Your customers occasionally have changes in their lives. They lose jobs or businesses; they have marital problems; or they have any number of other difficulties. Some individuals are deadbeats who never intend to pay. Regardless of the reason, some payments won't be made in the agreed fashion.

It is necessary to pay careful attention to overdue receivables. Fine wine is said to improve with age. Overdue payments do not. The longer an account remains past due, the less likely you are to collect it and the less valuable it is to a bank.

You must inquire quickly about missed payments and repeatedly urge that they be made. If you can't get cash, repossession of the property may be in order. A poor credit and collections policy can be a drain on even the most successful company.

A persuasive secretary or clerk can often take care of such matters until the lending part of your operation grows substantially. At that time, you may want to consider hiring a tactful (and perhaps large) person to keep all payments up to date, repossess inventory, and perform similar tasks.

In one recent case, a midwestern business hired as its collection representative a person who was skillful in dealing with those who were behind in their payments. In the first two weeks of his employment, collection of delinquent accounts increased by 1800 percent. A large drain on cash flow stopped.

If it looks as though it will be impossible for you to collect or repossess, turn the note over to a lawyer or professional collection agency. They will take a sizeable chunk of the amount collected, but at least you may get *something*. Don't be concerned that a person whose debt you turn over to such an agency will never buy from you again. Unless he is having only temporary financial reverses, any sale you make to him in the future would give you a loss. You can live without that type of customer.

If you earn the reputation of running a business which does not make all attempts to collect delinquent accounts, you'll have more and more purchases by people who have no intention of ever paying.

Occasional Sales of Personal Property

Although many installment sales are of inventory, others are sales of equipment, vehicles, and other productive personal property which a business no longer wants. These can include sales of trucks, radio equipment, computers, office furniture, or whatever—occasional, not regular, sales of "personal" property.

The profit to be included in a year's tax return is figured very much like it is for regular sales of personal property. For example, if you sell your business truck for $5,000, you might take $500 down and receive another $500 in the year of the sale. You might ask for another $1,000 per year for the next four years. If your cost or other basis in the item was $3,000, you have a $2,000 profit on the entire deal, and a 40 percent gross profit rate ($2,000 profit, divided by the $5,000 price).

A)	Sale Price	$5,000
	Cost of the Item Sold	3,000
B)	Your Gross Profit	$2,000
	Gross Profit Rate (B divided by A)	40%

So, 40 percent of each payment is assumed to be profit. If you receive $1,000 of payments each year, 40 percent, or $400, of each payment is shown on your tax return every year as profit from the sale of the truck.

Amount Received This Year	$1,000
× Gross Profit Rate	× 40%
Taxable Amount	$ 400

Profits from regular sales of inventory are included in your tax return as ordinary income. They receive no preferential treatment. It is possible, however, that an occasional sale of personal property can result in a long-term capital gain.

Tax law says specifically that *depreciable* business property can't be a capital asset. So, the truck in the above example is not a capital asset. Assume, instead, that the property had been an investment diamond, shares of stock, or a parcel of investment land (capital assets) which you'd owned for more than 12 months and one day. Each dollar of profit you placed on your tax return would be long-term capital gain.

In the above example, 40 percent, or $400, of each year's $1,000 payments were shown as profit. If each of these $400 amounts were a long-term capital gain (and you were showing them on your individual, not your corporate, tax return), another 60 percent, or $240, of the $400 profit would escape taxation because of favorable treatment. Only $160 per year would actually be taxed.

Amount Received This Year	$1,000
× Gross Profit Rate	× 40%
Taxable Amount (Long-Term Capital Gain)	$ 400
Less: Amount Which Escapes Tax (60% of Gain)	240
Amount Taxed to You	$ 160

When the sale of an item doesn't result in a long-term capital gain, the profit portion of each payment is fully taxed as ordinary income like profits, commissions, or salaries. Any interest you receive for carrying the note is also ordinary income, even if other gains on payments received are long-term capital gains. Losses on the sale of assets sold on the installment basis are placed on your tax return in the year of the sale; they are not postponed.

Sales of Real Estate

The installment sales method may be used for a sale of real estate either by a person who rarely sells his property, or by one who regularly sells parcels. The rules are virtually the same as those for casual sales of personal property.

When the profit portion of each payment is a long-term capital gain, only 40 percent of it is taxed. If it is not a long-term capital gain, all of the profit is taxed, as is any interest paid to you for carrying the note. Losses on sales of real estate aren't postponed, even though payments are received over several years. Losses are placed on your tax return in the year of the sale.

Keep the Note

Once an installment sale has been properly completed, and you are being taxed only when payments are received, you must be careful what you do with the note from the person who bought your property. Tax law says that virtually any disposal of an installment note causes you to be taxed on part or all of the gain you haven't yet put on your tax return. The amount of the gain taken to your tax return would be the sale price or fair market value of the note, less any cost of the property covered by the note which you have not yet received.

For example, let's say that you sold a piece of land for $5,000, taking $1,000 down and $1,000 each year for the next four years. You paid $2,000 for the property when you bought it, so 40 percent ($2,000 cost divided by $5,000 sale price) of each payment is return of your cost.

$$\frac{\text{Cost of Property (\$2,000)}}{\text{Sales Price of Property (\$5,000)}} = \begin{array}{c}40\% \text{ of each payment is} \\ \text{return of cost}\end{array}$$

If you sell the note when $3,000 is still owed to you, 40% of the $3,000, or $1,200, is your unrecovered cost. Let us say a bank is willing to give you only $2,800 for your $3,000 note. If so, you'd have a gain of $1,600 ($2,800, less your $1,200 of unrecovered cost) for your tax return that year. No further gain would be reported on note payments because you would not get any more payments.

Selling Price of the Note	$2,800
Cost of Property You've Not Yet Recovered (40% × $3,000 note balance)	1,200
Gain Taxed if You Sell the Note Now	$1,600

Of course, selling the note for more or less than $2,800 would give you a larger or smaller taxable gain than $1,600.

If you find yourself in need of cash, you can probably borrow money, using the note as collateral. This will raise the cash you need, in most cases, without causing taxes to be due on the entire remaining gain.

But don't sell the note, or use it as down payment on property, or do anything else with it. Your carefully negotiated installment sale will become a regular taxable sale with almost any type of disposition of the note.

Pyramiding With Installment Notes

Something that you cannot have if you sell your property—even with the installment method—is continued participation in its increase in value. The appreciation in worth of a piece of real estate, for example, will no longer go to the seller. His asset (a mortgage note) is now locked into a specific amount of dollars and won't increase in value.

What can you do to protect yourself against inflation after you sell your asset with the installment method?

Using the mortgage note as collateral, you can borrow cash from a lending institution. Then you can invest the proceeds in other property which will increase in value.

A banker will not usually loan the full face value of your note, because he wants a margin of safety in case the debtor defaults. Fortunately, however, an installment sale often results in a combined down payment and note which is larger than the cash you'd receive from an outright sale. By providing the financing, you can frequently get a higher price for what is being sold. "Points" demanded by lenders and your closing costs are almost always less when you provide financing to the buyer.

Some individuals may even be able to battle inflation *better* by selling property they currently own with the installment method and reinvesting the proceeds in other property. Assume, for example, that a farmer has $80,000 of equity in a $100,000 ranch, with the other $20,000 being owed to a bank as a mortgage note.

Value of the Property	$100,000
Mortgage Note Owed	20,000
Owner's Equity	$ 80,000

Assuming the ranch increases in value by 10 percent, or $.0,000, during a year, the owner's net worth goes up by $10,000. If his net worth is $80,000, this increase adds 12½ percent to it ($10,000 increase, divided by $80,000 net worth).

Value of the Property	$100,000
× Rate of Appreciation	× 10%
Increase in Owner's Net Worth	$ 10,000
Percentage Increase in Owner's Net Worth ($10,000 divided by $80,000 net worth)	12½%

If the farmer decided to sell his property for $100,000 under the installment method he might get, for example, a $15,000 down payment and a $65,000 mortgage note. The buyer would assume the remaining $20,000 mortgage on the ranch.

Sale Price of the Property	$100,000
Existing Mortgage Assumed	20,000
Owner's Equity	$ 80,000
Cash Down Payment by Buyer	15,000
Mortgage Note to Seller	$ 65,000

Let's say that a bank would lend the farmer $45,000 on his $65,000 note. If so, he'd then have total cash of $60,000 ($15,000 down payment plus $45,000 of loan proceeds).

The buyer of the farm will make interest and principal payments to the farmer on his $65,000 note. These should more than cover payments on the farmer's new $45,000 debt.

With the $60,000 of cash, the farmer might buy a $240,000 income-producing property which could increase in value by 10 percent, or $24,000 per year. Rents from the new property would make all mortgage payments on it. With the ranch, his net worth would have changed by $10,000, or 12½ percent, each year. But the percentage increase on his former equity of $80,000 is now 30 percent ($24,000 divided by $80,000). He would now receive the benefit of increases in value of the $240,000 property, rather than a $100,000 parcel.

Value of the New Property	$240,000
× Rate of Appreciation	× 10%
Increase in Owner's Net Worth	$ 24,000
Percentage Increase in Owner's Net Worth ($24,000 divided by $80,000 net worth)	30%

As soon as his equity in the new property warrants, the farmer can again sell on the installment basis and borrow against the new note to purchase an even larger asset. In this way, he keeps the rate of return on his equity at a higher level than if he simply leaves his equity in the same property. As you saw in earlier chapters, a consistently high rate of compound growth can cause a phenomenal pyramiding effect to take place on capital. For example, if the farmer can make his $80,000 grow at only 20 percent compounded annually for the next 14 years, it will turn into $1,000,000 in that brief time.

Important Points

When compared with other types of transactions, installment sales have both advantages and disadvantages. The decision made in any single case will depend on the desires of the seller and an analysis of all the other economic and tax factors involved.

An installment sale can offer you several advantages over a conventional sale, such as 1) postponement of income taxes, 2) a possible higher sale price for the property you're selling, and 3) good interest income on the balance owed to you.

Since you are not taxed until cash is received, your business can build up its total assets faster than if sales were completely taxable when made. You are still paying taxes, but higher assets are shown to bankers and others because taxes are paid later, rather than sooner. You have an interest-free loan from Uncle Sam.

Tax law provides you with three types of installment sales—one for regular sales of inventory, another for occasional sales of personal property, and a third for sales of real estate. If you aren't able to dispose of an item with one of the tax-free methods explained in other chapters, one of these types of installment sales should help you keep your taxes on the sale at a minimum.

Although your natural inclination may be to get all your cash at the time of the sale, you may be able to raise all the operating funds you need by 1) borrowing on the receivables you have from your customers, 2) raising prices, 3) charging interest rates which are higher than your bank asks of you, and 4) paying close attention to your credit and collections policy.

You must be cautious about disposing of installment notes from customers. If you need cash, it would probably be better to borrow on a note than to sell it. The sale of a note would result in a gain for the year you sell it.

Even though you can no longer participate in the increase in value of property after you sell it, you may be able to use the cash down payment and note you receive to pyramid your equity to a much higher level. Borrowing on the note and reinvesting the proceeds in an inflation-resistant asset may cause your net worth to continue to grow nicely.

Whatever method you choose for selling an asset or assets, you should make the decision only after giving careful thought to *all* factors—especially defending yourself effectively against inflation and saving as much taxes as possible each day. The installment sales method can help you do both.

PART SIX

Staying One Step Ahead of The IRS

22

Tax Traps to Avoid

Tax law has often been put together in piecemeal fashion. Since the early part of this century, Congress has been attempting to make allowance for every imaginable circumstance in which a business or individual could find itself or himself. Loopholes have been plugged and others opened. Economic objectives have been encouraged. Rules have been passed or deleted at the insistence of special interest groups.

To make things worse, the law changes daily as the IRS, courts, and other institutions put forth pronouncements and decisions.

Tax law is a maze.

And it is entirely possible for a business owner to fall into any number of tax traps hidden in the maze.

Some of these pitfalls have been set for those who appear to be trying to get away with something shady. Other snares may cause serious problems for people whose intentions are entirely honorable.

It is important that you be aware of several of the more common traps so that you can avoid the circumstances which lead to each. So, let's take a look at how you could fall into traps and what you can do to stay out of them.

Excess Investment Interest

The excess investment interest rule may seem to be more a "limit" than a trap. But it could prevent you from deducting part of the interest you've paid in the year you pay it. It's the rule, not your honorable intentions or lack of familiarity with tax law which will govern the result.

How to Shift Your Income

It was common, years ago, for people to borrow large amounts of money which enabled them to own investments such as shares of stock or vacant land. The interest they paid would be a deduction against the profits or income they earned elsewhere. So, their taxes were lowered.

Then, the investments were sold in later years— usually for long-term capital gains. It was an excellent way of turning this year's unprotected ordinary income (profits, salary, commissions, or other earnings) into some other year's capital gain. And, to an extent, it can still be done.

Assume, for example, that you buy a vacant piece of land for $50,000 and finance it at 10 percent annual interest. You would pay roughly $5,000 of interest in the first full year of ownership.

This $5,000 would be deducted against the profits of your business, reducing them and lowering your tax bill. At the same time, the vacant lot should go up in value by at least $5,000. (If it were not going to increase in value by at least your carrying costs, you wouldn't buy it, would you?)

So, your profits—unprotected ordinary income—are reduced. And your investment goes up by the same amount or more. In essence, you're transferring income from one place to another.

But the rise in value of your investment is not taxed until it is sold. Even then, it will probably be taxed leniently with long-term capital gain rates. So, you are turning ordinary income into long-term capital gain.

Limit on Interest Deductions

Congress decided that a little of this would be all right. However, too much just was not acceptable. As usual, the "problem" was solved with legislation. The rules on excess investment interest limit the amount of interest an individual can deduct on money he's borrowed to own investment property (shares of stock, vacant land, precious metals, and others).

These rules do not normally apply to interest on money you have borrowed to own business property or income-producing real estate. Neither do they bother people who pay less than $10,000 in interest annually in order to carry investments.

But they *can* affect those who pay more than $10,000 a year in interest to own investments. And they can also be a problem for people who are, in essence, guaranteed a specific return on their income-producing real estate or who do not participate in its management.

Basically, your annual deduction for investment interest is limited to $10,000. This limit can be increased by any net income from your investments and a few other items. But many investments produce negligible income, adding little to the $10,000 figure.

Postpone Income, Not Deductions

If you go over your limit, any interest above that point can't be deducted on your current year's tax return. You can only carry it over and try to deduct it in the next year. So, you are paying cash this year for a deduction which is postponed until next year or some later year—an expensive process. Your cash should be used to buy deductions and credits you can use *now*.

What is the best solution?

Don't worry about interest you pay in order to own assets you use in your business. These financing costs should be deductible without question. But think carefully before you buy your next investment. Is the total interest you pay to carry investments already approaching $10,000 per year? If it is, you may want to either pay cash for this investment or to buy something else which your business will be able to use in its operations.

There is no point in paying hard-earned cash for interest you can't deduct until later, when there are all kinds of tax breaks which your cash can generate for use this year.

Sales to Related Parties

Most sales and purchases of assets occur between disinterested parties in "arm's-length" transactions. Neither side gives the other anything. Each negotiates the best possible deal for himself.

Gains on these sales are taxable and losses are deductible.

Occasionally, an asset is sold by someone to a "related" buyer. Any gain is usually taxable on such a sale. But a loss may not be deductible at all.

Why?

With all the "arm's-length" buyers in the U.S., the IRS wonders why the sale was made to a related party. If the asset was sold at a loss, why was it sold to a related taxpayer, rather than to some unknowing outsider? Most people would be careful not to sell a bad investment to a relative.

So, the IRS assumes that hidden motives are present—you just made the sale to generate a loss for your tax return, but you believe that the investment will go up in value and want to keep it in the family. Otherwise, the item would have been sold to a disinterested, unrelated buyer.

Who are these buyers who can stop you from deducting your loss?

Your Related Taxpayers

Roughly, tax law sees your spouse, brothers and sisters, ancestors and descendants (parents, grandparents, children, grandchildren), and any corporation of which you own more than 50 percent as being related to you.

"Constructive ownership" makes the situation a little more complicated. If any of your related parties owns shares of stock in a corporation, *you* are presumed to own those shares. So, if you and your brother each own 30 percent of the stock in a corporation, that corporation is one of your related taxpayers—you're seen as owning 60 percent of its stock. Selling an asset at a loss to the corporation would yield the same result as selling it at a loss to your brother. The "loss" would not be deductible.

Let's say, for example, that you sell a vacant lot (for which you'd paid $30,000) to this corporation for a price of $20,000. It might appear that you have a $10,000 loss ($20,000 sale price, less $30,000 cost). But you do not have any loss. You may be certain in your own mind that the property *has* declined in value. But the IRS is just as certain that you are keeping the land in the family for some reason. If you had truly wanted a loss, you could've sold it to an outsider.

Salvaging a "Lost" Loss

Fortunately, the related taxpayer who buys your asset may be able to make use at some later date of the loss you couldn't put on your tax return.

Assume that your corporation sells that vacant lot for $50,000. Normally, the company would show a $30,000 gain ($50,000 sale price, less the $20,000 amount it paid you for the property). But tax law permits the corporation to use your previously disallowed loss against that gain. The $30,000 gain is cut back to $20,000 by using your $10,000 disallowed loss against it.

When you truly need a loss to save taxes on your tax return, sell an asset which has declined in value to some disinterested party. If you want to keep the property in your family, remember that you must generate a loss or deduction somewhere else. At least you won't suddenly find yourself with a "lost" loss and a surprise tax bill.

Unreasonable Compensation

As you saw in Chapter 9, one way you may be able to cut your tax bill is to operate your business as a corporation. For certain levels of income, corporate tax rates are lower than the rates an individual would pay. The result can be less tax owed to Uncle Sam.

But cash or other property drawn out of your corporation as dividends can be taxed twice—once when the corporation earns profits and again when you receive them from the business.

This is rarely a problem with Subchapter S corporations (Chapter 12). Income is taxed directly to you, rather than to a Sub S. If cash is paid out to you as it is earned, you avoid double taxation.

Similarly, you may be able to "milk" cash out of your regular (non-Sub S) corporation so that it is deducted by the business and taxed only to you. The most common methods of doing this are to pay yourself salary for your labor or rent, royalties, or interest for the use of your own property.

Taking cash out in these ways means that the earnings you receive are taxed only once. These funds won't be later paid out by the corporation and taxed to you again as dividends.

This is where the problem of "unreasonable compensation" can arise.

How Much Are Your Services Worth?

The IRS wants to place a limit on the amount you can drain out of your corporation as salary and have taxed only once. If they figure you've squeezed out too much, they will call part of it "salary" and the remainder "dividends." Your corporation can deduct salary, but not dividends. So, the amount paid to you as dividends is taxed once to the corporation, then again to you.

Let's say that you let your corporation pay you a $100,000 salary for a year. Then the IRS successfully argues that your effort was worth only $60,000 during the year. If so, you had every right to pay the other $40,000 to yourself ($100,000 total, less $60,000 of salary)—but as dividends, not salary. Suddenly, your corporation can deduct only $60,000, not $100,000. Yet you are taxed on the entire $100,000 you've received.

It may not seem fair, but it is true.

Since you probably do not wish to draw cash out of your

corporation if it's going to be taxed twice, you will want to be familiar with how "reasonable" is distinguished from "unreasonable" compensation.

How Much Is Reasonable?

To figure out what your maximum salary should be, the IRS looks at several factors in your business, such as:

1) How much work did you do during the year? Did you put in 40-hour work weeks or did somebody else run the business?

2) What type of work did you do? Were you the manager or did you just occasionally help set overall business policies?

3) How much were the salaries of people doing comparable work in similar businesses?

4) Did you give yourself a huge raise over the prior year or just a reasonable increase?

5) If the corporation earned a great deal of money during the year, did you pay yourself at least *some* dividends (taxed twice) in addition to salary?

6) Do your personal qualifications (education and experience) justify the salary you paid yourself for the year?

Although the IRS may weight some of these questions more heavily than others and can even bring up additional factors, they give you the basic idea. The government wants you to pay yourself what you're worth—and no more. Any additional payments should be taxed as dividends.

And it is not just *your* salary they'll look at. If you are trying to cut your overall tax burden by paying relatives salaries for doing next to nothing, the IRS will take a hard look at these cash outlays. You may find that you're better off to save taxes by splitting your business with relatives (Chapter 6). This can help you reach the same goal with fewer problems of unreasonable compensation.

In addition to a reasonable salary, you may be able to draw cash out of your corporation by renting property or equipment to it. When you hit your limit there, you may wish to concentrate on deductible fringe benefits (Chapter 11). Fringe benefits won't draw cash out of the business, but they can often provide other rewards without the problem of double taxation.

Constructive Dividends

As with unreasonable compensation, the IRS may use the idea of "constructive dividends" to cause other benefits you receive to be declared dividends—taxable to you, but not deductible by the corporation.

One of these sensitive areas is rent on property you own. If your corporation pays you more rent than you could otherwise earn on an asset, the IRS may try to call part of the rent a "dividend."

Another dangerous item is a loan from your corporation to you. When it is informal (no signed note, interest rate, due date, or collateral), it certainly can appear that you had no intention of repaying the note. The IRS may be able to convince themselves that you gave yourself a dividend, not a loan. Although loans aren't taxable to you, dividends you receive are.

And what about bargains your corporation gives you? Is it renting items to you (for non-business purposes) at low rates or letting you use them for free? Has it sold property to you at a below-market price? If so, these bargains have the same result that you'd see if you paid full price for what you got, then received part or all of your cash back from the corporation. The cash returned to you would be a dividend.

There are plenty of tax breaks available without becoming involved with a constructive dividend. Don't let the IRS have reason to think that you tried to sneak some cash or property out of your corporation. If you want to save taxes on business profits, other deductions can give you a more straightforward reduction of your tax bill.

Accumulated Earnings Tax

In order to keep from being taxed twice on dividends, it's tempting to just leave the cash in your corporation. Net earnings are taxed once to the corporation (after you drain out as much as you reasonably can in salary and other payments) and then you just let profits accumulate in the business.

But the IRS doesn't want you to keep more earnings in the corporation than your business really needs in order to operate. Leaving profits in the corporation means that you do not pay as much taxes as you would if you paid yourself dividends each year.

So, the IRS can apply what is known as the "accumulated earnings tax." This tax arises when you build up more earnings in your corporation than it needs in order to function. The IRS figures you've left profits in the corporation so that you would not be required to pay taxes on them as dividends.

Before the accumulated earnings tax comes into play, you can normally build up a $250,000 accumulation. In addition, your corporation may need a considerable earnings accumulation to satisfy needs which can arise. You may want to retire debt, acquire more assets, set aside funds for contingencies, increase your working capital, or take care of other requirements. But, whatever you see as your needs, they must be reasonable, feasible, specific, definite, and well-documented (in your corporate minutes and elsewhere).

How the Tax Works

When you build up earnings beyond what you can justify, the accumulated earnings tax can take 27½ percent of the first $100,000 of excess and 38½ percent beyond that.

For example, let us say that you are able to justify $300,000 of accumulated corporate earnings, but you have tacked $250,000 on top of that (a total of $550,000 of profits retained in the business). The accumulated earnings tax will take 27½ percent of the first $100,000 of this excess, or $27,500 and 38½ percent of the next $150,000, or $57,750.

Total Corporate Profits Accumulated	$550,000
Amount You Can Justify	300,000
Excess	$250,000
First $100,000 of excess	$100,000
× Tax Rate	× .275
Tax on First $100,000 of Excess	$ 27,500
Remainder of Excess ($250,000 − $100,000)	$150,000
× Tax Rate	× .385
Tax on Remainder of Excess	$ 57,750

Your accumulated earnings tax totals $85,250 for the year. You didn't pay the profits out as taxable dividends, so the IRS will just hit your corporation with an extra tax.

How can this be avoided?

Justify Your Accumulation of Earnings

Be absolutely certain that you have a well-documented, believable reason for every nickel of earnings you've kept in your corporation. And be sure that your reasons are documented before or during the accumulation, not afterward when it starts to look as though the accumulated earnings tax could hurt you.

Relate these reasons to your current line of business. If you plan to invest in assets which are not related to your corporation's basic operations, to loan money to yourself, or to put the earnings into other unrelated projects, you will be looking at the accumulated earnings tax.

Numerous corporations have accumulated millions, even hundreds of millions, of dollars in earnings without being bothered by this extra tax. So, there's no need to spend sleepless nights thinking about it. But be certain, if your corporation's accumulated profits are more than $250,000, that you can demonstrate a clear need for keeping those earnings in the business rather than paying them out as dividends.

Personal Holding Company Tax

Often a high-tax-bracket individual sees that he could pay less tax by forming a corporation and putting part or all of his investments into it. Corporate tax rates may be far less than the rates which are applied on his individual income tax return. By putting his investments into a corporation, he'd just pay corporate taxes on the income and let remaining profits build up in the corporation.

Although the accumulated earnings tax is a possibility in such cases, the IRS can apply a different tax—the personal holding company tax. This penalty is especially used when most of the earnings of a corporation are "passive" income from investments, rather than profits from actively running a business.

When the Tax Applies

You can run afoul of the personal holding company tax when:

1) At least 60 percent of your corporation's income comes from dividends, interest, royalties, rents, and certain other types of passive income *and*

2) One to five people own more than half the value of the corporation's stock during the last half of the year.

When your corporation falls under one of these tests, but not the other, you won't see the personal holding company tax applied.

For example, let's say that you are manufacturing and selling wood products. Very little, if any, of your income is described in 1) above. So, you do not own a personal holding company.

Or assume that 11 people equally own the corporation (roughly nine percent ownership each). In this case, five people could only own 45 percent of the business. This would keep you from coming under 2) above.

Assuming that you meet both tests, though, you've got a personal holding company and may owe both your regular corporate income tax *and* a 50 percent personal holding company tax.

If this seems severe, that's because it *is*. The IRS simply does not want corporations to fall into the personal holding company category.

Minimizing or Avoiding the Tax

Fortunately, the penalty is applied after you subtract dividends from income. Under certain conditions, you can even pay dividends after your corporation's tax year closes.

But, whenever possible, it's best to just stay as far away from personal holding company status as possible. If your corporation has considerable income such as interest and dividends from investments, you'll want to either keep those earnings to less than 60 percent of the total or drain them out as salaries, rents, dividends, or other payments.

Extra caution is required when you are starting or winding up a business and a large part of your assets is temporarily invested in interest- or dividend-producing securities. Without the ability to generate "active" business income, you could quickly find yourself over a barrel as "passive" income makes up more than 60 percent of earnings.

Substance Over Form

When you do everything by the rules, but the IRS believes you're trying to get around part of the law, Uncle Sam will bring up the idea of "substance over form." He'll claim that the form of what you did was okay, but that the substance of your action was to do something entirely different.

Assume that you own a piece of land you bought for $40,000. You want to take a loss on the property, but you'd also like to keep it in the family. You are aware that the rules concerning sales to related parties make reaching both these goals impossible. So, you sell the parcel to your trusted friend, Adam, for $30,000. This gives you a $10,000 loss.

According to your wishes, Adam then sells the land to your brother, Bill, for $30,000. It appears that you've gotten your loss *and* kept the property in the family.

But the IRS shrinks all this down to a single step. The IRS sees only a single sale—one to a related party. The government won't allow you to deduct the loss.

It is best to avoid transactions which look as though they could be shrunk down to an entirely different transaction. You'll only give the government the idea that your affairs need further study. There are just too many straightforward tax breaks to become involved with a substance over form argument.

Important Points

Tax law is too large and disorganized for any single person to have a perfect grasp of every detail. It's not surprising that someone who spends almost all his time running a business (instead of studying tax law) could fall into one or more of the traps hidden in the maze of rules and regulations. In order to steer away from them, you need to be aware of the more common pitfalls.

Unless you've borrowed money to carry one or more large investments, you probably won't have difficulty with the excess investment interest rule. But if this rule were to apply to your situation, it would mean that your cash expenditures (for interest) were not generating the deductions that they could. Investment interest above $10,000 per year would be postponed for possible deduction in later years.

Remember not to sell anything at a loss to a related party unless you have plenty of other deductions for the year. Your loss may be disallowed and you can find yourself paying taxes on income you thought was sheltered by the loss.

One of the reasons for incorporating your business is to take advantage of lower corporate income tax rates. The drawback to this is that cash paid out to you by the corporation as dividends is taxed again upon receipt.

Although dividends can't be deducted by your corporation, salary, rent, interest, and royalties can. You may be tempted to draw as much cash out as you can in these forms. This is an excellent way to accomplish your goals as long as you do not use it in excess. If the IRS raises the questions of "unreasonable compensation" or "constructive dividends," you could find part of your corporate deductions turned into nondeductible dividends.

Your personal tax rates may be so high that you prefer to leave as much earnings in your corporation as possible. If so, you'll need reasonable, documented plans for using the funds retained in your business. Otherwise, you may set yourself up for the accumulated earnings tax.

Similarly, if most of your profits are "passive" earnings from investments and your corporation is owned by only a few people, the personal holding company tax could be applied.

And whenever it appears that you've done everything by the book in order to get around some tax rule, the IRS could employ the "substance over form" idea to get their way. A suspicious series of transactions can be collapsed in order to see what the result would've been with fewer steps.

Although the tax savings you may find by guiding your business near these traps seem attractive, the real cost (in terms of lost deductions and surprise tax bills) can often outweigh what you gain. There is little reason to take risks in order to save a few dollars when you can use relatively straightforward tax breaks to save much more.

Other chapters of this book explain numerous clear-cut ways to partially or completely eliminate your annual tax liability. With them, you will be more likely to have Uncle Sam's blessing and your own peace of mind.

23

How the IRS Catches Unreported Income

Many of the most famous criminals in the history of the U.S. have been imprisoned, not for racketeering or drug dealing, but for failing to pay taxes on the money they acquired illegally. This has happened because tax law says that income from *any* source (unless specifically exempted) is taxable. So, sales of drugs, bank robbery and embezzlement proceeds, and even cash found on the sidewalk and kept are all taxable.

But noted crime figures comprise only a small percentage of the individuals sentenced to prison for running afoul of the IRS. Most have just been average folks who "forgot" to show part or all of their income on a tax return or otherwise disobeyed the tax law.

And the total of people jailed is far less than the number who have barely managed to escape the IRS with expensive legal or accounting assistance and perhaps a fine. We all have an Uncle Frank or a friend of a friend who has had big tax trouble.

The business owner is especially tempted to use a variety of illegal means to cut taxes. Although courts believe firmly that each individual should use every deduction, credit, income exclusion, and anything else available to legally cut his tax bill, they object to falsifying deductions or leaving income off the tax return. In fact, the person who uses every legal loophole is *not* a "tax evader," but a "tax minimizer" or "tax avoider." Only "tax evaders" are looking for trouble.

Temptation for the Business Owner

Falsifying deductions isn't usually as attractive to business owners as hiding income. Almost everyone realizes that a cancelled check, paid invoice, or other document is needed to prove a deduction. But many people eventually see how easy it is to hide income. If the business deals mainly in cash, all the owner has to do is "skim" part of each day's receipts out of the cash register or cash box before they are deposited.

It may be hard to condemn people who do this. Each of us wants a fair return for money he gives up, and hardly anyone approves wholeheartedly of the way federal income taxes are used today. Periodic exposure of widespread welfare and food stamp fraud, large grants for seemingly ridiculous research projects, and foreign aid to countries who tend to waste it just reinforces our own doubts about the benefits we get for our tax dollars.

It is only natural that these disillusionments, when combined with an individual's instincts to look out first for his family and himself could lead many people to either fudge on deductions or to not report all of their income.

The IRS, however, has a job to do and is intent on doing it—even if someone has to go to a federal penitentiary. The IRS is charged with enforcing the tax law and can't have the luxury of sympathizing with those who leave income off their tax returns.

Common-Sense Investigation Techniques

Since it has an unusual job to do, the IRS has been given extra-ordinary powers to carry out its duties. People continually suggest that IRS authority goes beyond what is allowed in the U.S. Constitution. For many situations, however, the IRS doesn't need to go beyond common sense and ordinary records to catch an individual who evades taxes.

Business owners often leave an obvious trail because they are ignorant of the logical techniques used by the IRS, or because they think they will never be caught. In tax evasion, as in any other area of disobeying the law, ignorant or careless people are most likely to be caught.

What are the ways that the IRS has at its disposal to catch someone who does not put all his income on the tax return? Among the methods available, five loom large. These are (1) informants, (2) analysis of bank deposits, (3) the percentage method, (4) proof of expenditures more than reported income, and (5) detection of unexplained increases in net worth.

Informants

We read or hear every day of the arrest of some thief or killer because of a tip received from another individual who was aware of his guilt. The informant usually observed the act or was told about it by the person arrested. We might ask ourselves how the criminal could have been so careless as to allow the informant to find out.

Transferring the same situation to enforcing tax law, where a financial reward may be available to the informant, how can we expect an angry ex-spouse, disgruntled partner, or fired employee *not* to call the IRS? Even though a business owner may figure no one will object to his besting the IRS—and may be slightly proud of the fact that he has accomplished it—the informant has nothing to lose. And an informant's revenge may be very sweet as the real loser goes through expensive court fights, fines, and/or imprisonment.

What leads to the tax evader being turned in by the informant? Usually, the guilty party talks too much, or the informant is privy to the act of hiding income. Then, as happens in many interpersonal situations, the informant is disappointed in some way by the business owner. A timeless scenario repeats itself as an individual who has something to hide allows one too many people to find out.

If additional motivation is needed, the IRS may pay the informant up to ten percent of the extra taxes collected. The government is said to pay hundreds of thousands of dollars of such rewards each year.

A dentist was recently caught after his fired assistant told the IRS that part of his dental fees went unreported. Each fee went into his record books with one of two codes which indicated whether the fee would be placed on his tax return or left off. The dentist's problems were compounded by the fact that the unhappy former assistant knew this code.

The fact is that not showing taxable income on your return, even if it seems entirely justifiable, can be a federal crime. The more people who know about an individual's failure to report income, the greater is the probability that one of them will be an informant.

Analysis of Bank Deposits

Someone with only a small amount of bookkeeping or accounting training can examine your bank statement with deposits and cancelled checks, and tell you more than you presently know about yourself. He can see whether or not you are living beyond your means, how much you drink, how charitable you are, and how well you dress and eat. If he also has access to your tax return, he can determine whether or not you've made deposits which are left off your return.

Besides building an army of potential informants, one of the most ridiculous things people do is deposit income they do not report on their tax returns. Many folks still hold the false idea that bank checking and savings account statements are confidential documents which are only available to the bank and the depositor.

Whether or not we believe it is "right," government employees, including IRS agents, have ways of getting access to bank statements. In fact, law requires that deposits of cash over a specific amount be automatically reported by your bank to the federal government. Your bank records are permanent histories of your transactions and can be made available as evidence in an investigation.

Since smaller businesses and individuals often use the cash basis of reporting revenues (deposits equal revenues), it is easy to see if total deposits for the year equal the total shown on the tax return. For businesses on the accrual method, the matching process is more involved, but usually is not difficult for a trained person.

If bank records show more revenue than does the tax return, the difference may be due to transfers from one bank account to another, tax-free gifts received, other nontaxable amounts such as life insurance proceeds—or hidden income.

Proof

One mistaken belief that many people have is that they are innocent until proven guilty. You sometimes hear, "Let the IRS try to prove such and such." They probably pick this up from watching courtroom dramas on television, not from reading tax law.

Oddly enough, the *owner* of a bank account usually must prove that deposits he makes (and leaves off his tax return) are *not* income. He is not able to humorously watch the IRS try to prove that they *are* income. This fact can make a big difference in who is relaxed during the examination of bank records.

If frequent deposits have been made to an account, with few of them bearing accurate identification, a larger amount can wind up being taxed as income than even ought to be. If you cannot prove that deposits aren't income, then they may be called income by a court.

Common Sense

Like the person who allows potential informants to know that he is hiding income, the fellow who deposits taxable sums which don't reach his tax return is leaving an easy trail to follow. He may get lucky and never have his bank account examined. But he may not be so fortunate.

Those who have frequent unusual transactions, who are thought to participate in illegal activities, or who are found by the IRS to be cheating in other areas are especially ripe for a check of their bank accounts. And an informant increases the likelihood even further.

In fact, it is rumored that some people who participate in illegal activities also own legitimate businesses so that they can report illegal receipts through their legal companies. This is said to be especially common in southern states into which large quantities of illegal drugs are smuggled. Earnings from drug sales, for example, may be taxed as though they are dry cleaning, supermarket, movie, or restaurant income. The drug dealers may still be liable for arrest by other branches of government, but at least the IRS has what it wants—the income taxes.

The Percentage Method

Suppose that you have few potential informants and never deposit income which you don't plan to report on your tax return. Is there any other way in which a business owner can be caught for consistently taking cash out of the cash register and not reporting it?

The IRS has percentages of gross and net profits on sales for a variety of businesses, taken either from other enterprises or from your own old returns. All the government has to do is figure out your current sales and apply these percentages to find out whether you regularly skim cash before depositing the rest.

Naturally, only moderate or large amounts taken out regularly would be likely to show up, and a greater burden of proof may fall on the IRS in these cases than when your bank account is examined. But it is surprising how many cases can be proven with solid evidence provided with percentages.

Take, for instance, a car wash. Almost all of the receipts of these businesses are in cash. It must be very tempting to leave a large portion of the receipts off the owner's tax return. But all the government has to do to get total sales is to divide the water or soap bills by an average amount used per automobile, then multiply by the revenue per vehicle. Or they can count the average number of cars that use the facility on various days, then multiply by estimated revenue per auto.

Once they have an estimate of sales that will stand up in court, they multiply by the time-honored gross profit and net profit ratios for car washes and look at the difference between their figures and the numbers on the owner's tax return. A small difference may not provide the proof needed, but a large discrepancy could be very embarrassing.

Similarly, the number of customers of a restaurant can be counted on several days and an estimate of sales made by multiplying customers by average charges. The same principle applies to many other businesses which have regular daily sales.

This type of failure to report revenue is probably more difficult to discover and prove than that which is found in bank records, especially when only a small percentage is not reported or when sales fluctuate dramatically. The fact remains, however, that the IRS may be able to prove its case in many circumstances. The testimony of an informant can make the proof even more solid.

Expenditures More Than Reported Income

Spending money which is not reported on the tax return can sometimes enable the government to prove guilt. This is especially the case for people who are consistent in their shopping habits. One actual recent situation concerned a very prominent politician who allegedly accepted bribes. Agents were apparently able to determine from visits to just a few clothing stores, automobile dealerships, and other retail outlets that he spent considerably more than what he said was his income. The result was a national scandal.

If, for instance, an individual's reported income is $50,000, but he spends $75,000, or $100,000, where does this extra cash come from? If he says it comes from savings, the withdrawals should show up on savings account statements. If gifts are involved, the alleged donors could be questioned in court.

Even if it is never deposited to a bank account, the untaxed income is more or less "deposited" with shops selling different types of merchandise. All the IRS has to do is check the size and regularity of these purchases to establish that income is above that shown on the tax return.

Unexplained Increases In Net Worth

Similar to the investigation for spending more than reported income, the unexplained increase in net worth method compares the net worth of a person at the beginning and end of a period. Net worth, of course, is assets minus liabilities.

Let's say that the net worth of an individual at the beginning of a year is $50,000, and is $150,000 at the end of the same year. We can determine the number for each date by adding up his assets such as bank accounts, clothing, automobiles, houses, and investments, and subtracting his debts. What we see, then, is a $100,000 increase in net worth. If he also spent $25,000 on living expenses such as food, gasoline, doctor bills, and taxes, his total income for the year should have been $125,000. If his tax return shows income of $50,000, the extra amount may be income he "forgot" to put on his tax return.

The more obvious examples of unexplained increases in net worth sometimes occur in locales where drug traffic is highest. People who work for minimum wage during the week can finish the year with a new brick home. What can the IRS assume other than unreported income?

This was brought vividly to the public's attention as television camera crews and reporters recently accompanied agents on a raid to confiscate the personal effects of a suspected drug-smuggling family in a southern state. But the "net worth" method can just as easily be used on the owner of a legitimate business.

Important Points

Although many individuals are unhappy with what their tax dollars buy and prefer to spend the money on themselves and their families, the IRS has a job to do. Informants, random investigations of other areas of your tax situation, or audits of people with whom you do business can sometimes trigger a thorough examination of your own financial affairs.

Business owners *are* tempted not to report all revenues on their tax returns. But if the amount left off the return is large enough, the government may be able to make a solid case before a judge. An individual who deposits his unreported income in a checking or savings account is giving the government assistance in his own conviction. He is providing excellent records which *he* must then prove do not show hidden income.

If cash is taken out of the till before the remainder is counted and deposited, the IRS may be able to make a case with its industry percentages of gross and net profits on sales. Agents must sit in a restaurant long enough to establish the average number of customers per day and average customer payment, or observe a car wash to get an accurate daily usage rate. The percentages multiplied by gross income give estimated gross profit and net profit figures.

Even if an enterprise's records are destroyed, the IRS may be able to use its own observations to approximately reconstruct the information lost. The larger the discrepancy between figures, the more obvious it is that income was probably hidden.

Investigations of expenditures higher than reported income and unexplained increases in net worth may require considerable leg work by the IRS, and may be more appropriate in larger cases or where the government wishes to set an example. To verify excess expenditures, agents must discuss spending habits with the clothing stores, car dealerships, supermarkets, and other merchandisers where an individual shops. If the total that they find as having been spent exceeds by a good margin the income shown on his tax return, the excess had to come from some other source—probably unreported income.

Likewise, if the total of a person's increase in net worth, plus other expenditures, is substantially larger than income shown on his tax return, he may be asked to explain what caused the difference. If the extra cash didn't come from gifts or other nontaxable sources, hidden revenue may be the answer.

The presence of informants who are angry at an individual who has hidden income, and are familiar with his financial affairs, can complicate the situation by calling attention to him.

A business owner the IRS is investigating can hire any number of excellent lawyers who are experienced in these cases. Such attorneys may frequently be able to contest government evidence, and work out compromises with the IRS which, although expensive, can keep clients out of prison.

Even a great lawyer, however, may not be able to work a miracle. The person who builds an army of informants and/or provides an excellent trail for the IRS to follow in proving large amounts of unreported income may find himself an example for others. The IRS knows that nothing brings other potential tax evaders in line like reading about the conviction and sentencing of someone else who tried it.

24

Surviving and Appealing a Tax Audit

The foundation for a good tax savings program is 1) your familiarity with the tax breaks that are available and 2) your knowledge of when and how to use them. After you construct the foundation, you must use as many of these tax-cutting methods as you can.

But there is one more important aspect to consider.

Congress writes tax laws and gives the job of enforcing them to the IRS. Being aware of how to deal successfully with the IRS when they raise questions should be another part of your overall business ability.

You've got to be able to keep the tax breaks and cash that are rightfully yours.

Doing so does not mean that you are trying to "get away" with something shady. And this is not a chapter about how to avoid an organization that is "out to nail you."

The IRS *can* ask a court to fine or jail you. So can the Post Office. The IRS does have certain powers which other bureaucrats do not. But, in the majority of cases, dealing successfully with the IRS is about the same as doing so with any other government agency.

You'll want to follow the rules, be reasonable, and use your head.

What Happens to Your Tax Return?

When you mail your tax return, it goes to one of ten regional IRS Service Centers. You may have driven by such a facility. Each looks like an office complex or a factory. And that's exactly what it is—a factory which processes billions of pieces of financial data.

Your return is checked for accuracy, then fed into a computer terminal. A tape containing your data is then sent to Martinsburg, West Virginia, for storage.

If you send a check with your return, it will be deposited. If a refund is due, you will probably receive it. Cashing your check or sending you a refund says nothing about the IRS' future interest in your tax return.

The IRS has three years or more within which to audit you. And, in fact, most audits currently lag considerably behind the dates tax returns are filed.

Your Odds of Avoiding an Audit

The IRS computer takes a careful look at your tax return. Recent audits all over the U.S. have given the computer an idea of what the average should be for each type of deduction and credit for people in your income range. If the computer thinks that something on your return is way out of line (or too many items are a little high), the computer recommends you for a possible audit.

An IRS employee then normally evaluates your return from his own viewpoint to see if he agrees with the computer. If he doesn't, you probably will not be audited. If he does, you will.

What does the computer think is "too high?" The IRS resists giving out this information.

But it is known that your odds of being audited depend partly on each of a number of factors. How much income did you have during the year? Did you itemize? Do you have a business? If so, how large? Does your return show any unusual items such as a vacation home or large charitable contributions? The list is lengthy.

A certain number of random audits are performed each year on persons from all income groups. These are done for the purpose of keeping everybody honest and a little frightened.

A few audits are caused by an unusual event, such as an informant talking to the IRS about something you've done (Chapter 23) or your request for a refund of taxes you paid in past years.

The remainder of examinations occur because the computer is interested in you.

You'll notice that the idea behind all this is that of selecting for audit only a fraction of the total number of tax returns filed. Like all government agencies, the IRS works on a budget. The odds are *against* your being audited.

In fact, depending upon your income level, occupation, and other factors, the chances of your individual or corporate return being audited probably vary from a low of about one in a hundred to a high of about one in ten. The average may be one in thirty or forty. Some years it's one in fifty.

Put another way, the odds against your being audited are probably thirty or forty to one—possibly higher.

And when a return slips three years past its filing date, it will probably never be audited. For example, your 19 A tax return is due on April 15, 19 B (the next spring). On April 16, 19 E (three years later), your return is usually safe.

If the IRS can prove that you made a material error on your tax return, such as inadvertently leaving more than 25 percent of your income off the tax return, they have an additional three years within which to examine it.

If they can prove fraud, such as a deliberate omission of more than 25 percent of your income, the return can be audited at any time. Their time to examine it does not expire.

You Get a Letter From Uncle Sam

Let's say that something does trigger an audit. What then? Is it the end of the world?

Certainly not.

There are three basic types of "audits. '

First, you may just get a letter from the IRS computer telling you that you made a mistake on your tax return and asking you to send money. Many people panic when this happens and immediately send a check.

What you should do instead is determine whether or not the IRS is correct. If they are, send a check. If they are not, write them a letter and/or send additional tax forms required.

For example, when a financial institution pays you interest, it advises the IRS of that fact. If the interest does not appear on your tax return, you'll get a bill from the IRS. In such a case, there is probably no way around paying taxes you owe.

On the other hand, if you send a check with your tax return (rather than asking for a refund), you might get a bill for a penalty for underpayment of taxes. You may or may not actually owe this penalty. You can escape it under one of several exceptions with Form 2210.

Another type of audit is the "office" audit. The letter you receive will advise you which specific aspects of your tax return are being audited and will request that you bring your records supporting those parts of your return on a certain date to an IRS office.

The third type of audit is a "field" audit in which an IRS agent sets a date to look over portions of your records at your place of business. This normally occurs when bulky records are involved or other factors make it better for the IRS to visit you than the other way around.

If the date set for an audit is inconvenient, immediately call the IRS office named and request a change.

Whatever you do, don't ignore the letter. The result of an audit may lead to absolutely no change in your tax return. You may even receive a refund as a result of the examination.

But ignoring a request from this government agency is like ignoring one from any other agency. It makes them even more interested. You may compromise some of the tax savings you've worked so hard to achieve.

And this is one group of civil servants that can really make your life miserable. If you ignore them long enough, they may sell your business, house, car, and other property to pay what they believe to be your tax bill.

The idea that this might not be "fair" is irrelevant. It is a fact. And until the fact is changed by Congress, forward-looking people will take it into consideration.

What to Take With You to the Audit

Before you go to the audit, organize all of the information requested in the letter—no more, no less. If your tax return was prepared by someone else, meet with him and decide which of you will collect the data needed for the audit.

Remember, the burden of proof is on *you* to show that the return is correct. The IRS does not have to show that it isn't.

With this in mind, you may need to take accounting records, cancelled checks, receipts, brokerage documents, and other support to answer questions about the areas being examined by the IRS.

And organize your supporting paperwork so that you can immediately put your hands on any specific document for which the auditor asks. The less hesitation you have in answering questions and presenting proof, the better you'll look and the less time the audit will take.

Do not try to bury your auditor with cancelled checks, receipts, or other documents for which he does not ask. Just respond to his questions and provide him the proof he requires of you.

Who Should Accompany You?

If your tax return was signed jointly by you and your spouse, either of you can usually attend the audit. It is not necessary that both of you go.

In fact, if neither of you wishes to be at the audit, you can be represented by a qualified tax advisor to whom you've given written authorization to appear in your place.

If the letter advising you of the audit gives only a few, easily-answered areas of interest, you may wish to save the fee your tax advisor would charge by going to the audit alone. But, when your return is complicated and it appears that arguable issues could arise, think twice before you meet the IRS without your tax advisor.

Of course, some tax preparers promise to go with you to "explain" how your return was prepared. If you have a great deal at stake, you will want someone who is going to do more than just explain. You'll want a tax expert who will take your side of the case and effectively argue any points which are contested.

If you have chosen him wisely (Chapter 25), your advisor will convincingly justify each item on your return — including the valuable tax breaks you were so careful to use. He may be able to save you far more in taxes than the amount of his fee.

How to Act

If you face an audit with enthusiasm, you are a rare person. Most people feel anger, fear, or both. They may think that they have been singled out and accused of cheating on their tax returns. They are scared that intentional or inadvertent omissions will be discovered.

Try to remember that an auditor will normally concentrate on only a few areas of your return. Omissions you made won't necessarily be found. And, even if they are, the IRS wants your taxes much more than it wants to jail you. Only a tiny percentage of people audited are imprisoned.

So, before you go to the audit, decide in your own mind that you are a reasonable person who will be dealing with reasonable IRS personnel. Do not let your guard down. But don't prepare yourself to pick a fight.

If the examination is in IRS offices, start early so that you will be able to find a parking space and arrive on time.

Dress like a pauper or millionaire only if you are one.

Speak only when the IRS representative asks you a question and give only the answer requested. Just respond, then stop talking. If he goes with you to the audit, refer any difficult questions to your tax advisor.

When you are not accompanied by your tax advisor, politely argue your case when necessary, but stick to tax rules. Do not get into politics, "fairness," or what your neighbor deducts and gets away with.

Stay calm. You're dealing with a human being (who can make the audit tougher), not an impersonal government agency. Becoming antagonistic could cost you both time and money.

Do not get in a hurry or act as though you are too busy to be audited. The IRS alone will decide when the examination is finished.

A Word of Caution

What you should take to the audit, who should accompany you, and how you ought to act may change if one of three situations arises:

1) The agent conducting your audit indicates that the examina tion is anything other than routine.
2) Your auditor turns out to be a Special Agent or is accompanied by a Special Agent.
3) Your audit is being conducted by the IRS Criminal Division.

When any of these three circumstances is present, you will want to find the best tax advisor you can afford and strictly follow his advice before you tell the IRS anything. The government obviously has something serious in mind and anything you tell them could help them prepare a case against you.

Resolving and Appealing Disagreements

Tax law contains numerous gray areas and arguable points. But an IRS employee will peform an audit from the IRS viewpoint. You needn't automatically accept his findings.

If the two of you fail to agree, you can request an informal conference with the IRS Appeals Division. The person with whom you deal may be able to negotiate a settlement with you, because he'll be thinking in terms of savings costs by not going to court.

When this conference does not result in what you want, you can take the matter to court. At this point and beyond, you should be certain that you have an excellent reason not to simply reach a settlement with the IRS. Your legal costs will add up quickly.

Taking the Cheapest Way Out

While your tax advisor is helping you answer an auditor's questions, his meter is running. Since you are not working, your labor is being lost. So, you can add both these items to the cost of an audit.

If you appeal your case beyond the initial IRS audit to a conference and then go on to court, your total bill for accounting and legal expenses could be large.

Carefully weigh what you may possibly gain against the potential cost of these appeals. When the amount of taxes involved is sizeable and your tax advisor tells you that you will receive a much better deal on appeal, you may want to take the case further. But if yours is a hopeless cause or if the potential tax savings are smaller than the possible additional professional fees, it may be much cheaper just to pay your taxes and forget about it.

Important Points

The fact that a check you send with your tax return is cashed or that you receive a refund does not necessarily indicate that you will escape being audited. It means only that your return has been received, checked for accuracy, and fed into the IRS computer system for further reference.

The chances of your being audited in any given year are slim— normally thirty, forty, or even fifty to one. You increase your odds of being audited by making more money and by placing items on your tax return which the IRS computer sees as being different from the norm.

If the first indication you receive that the IRS is interested in your return is a request for cash, look into the matter as soon as possible.

You may owe additional taxes. On the other hand, you may be able to satisfy them merely by filing another tax form or forms.

When you are advised that you will be subjected to an office or field audit, start organizing your records which support the areas of your return which are to be examined. If your return is complex or you have reason to believe that this is not a routine inquiry, you will want to involve a qualified tax advisor the moment you receive the IRS letter.

Part of your success in dealing with the IRS will depend upon how well organized you are and how quickly you can provide documents requested during the examination. Your attitude and the way you act can also influence the outcome of an examination.

Try to remember that the purpose of an audit is just to make sure that your return complies with tax law. It isn't to call your honesty into question or to persecute you. At the worst, the IRS probably will only want some extra money. At the best, the audit will result in a refund of taxes to you.

If you aren't pleased with the result of the audit, carefully consider exactly what you can gain by appealing the initial IRS decision. Each situation is different. It is possible that you can work out a compromise with the IRS or even completely win your case by carrying it further. On the other hand, you could waste your own time and spend a great deal of money on a tax advisor for nothing. Take the cheapest way out.

The bottom line is that being aware of how to deal successfully with the IRS (or any other government agency) is just another aspect of running a profitable business. In particular, it is one specific part of your overall tax savings program.

And, as with all other aspects of your business, your goal should be to know as much as you can about each situation in which you find yourself and to keep the most cash you can at the least possible cost.

25

Choosing and Using a Tax Advisor

As you have seen, this book is full of tax-saving techniques for small businesses. The list of ways to keep from showing income on your tax return or to increase your deductions is a long one. All you have to do in order to benefit from these tax breaks is to make up your mind that you are going to do so, then arrange your affairs so that you qualify for the ones you choose.

People too often think about one part of a business—sales, purchasing, personnel management, or others—to the exclusion of the remaining areas. A business is like the human body. You cannot ignore any parts of it if you want to run it successfully. And taxes represent one such part—an important part.

Of course, you shouldn't think about taxes to the exclusion of all else. But this nation has decided that you *will* pay attention to tax rules if you want to keep your hands on enough cash to make your business successful. You can generate all the sales you want. And while you are out thinking about nothing but sales, the IRS will be happily draining your earnings out the back door.

You hire specialists to help you in areas of your business which are complicated. One of these areas is taxes. Although this book is written in an authoritative manner, it can't hope to point out all the dangers and opportunities in what you are doing each day. And tax laws change daily.

What you need is a loyal, qualified tax advisor. Such a person can keep you from falling into the IRS' waiting arms. He can help you save more dollars of taxes than the fees he charges you. He'll help you sleep at night, secure in the knowledge that you are doing just about everything you can to keep your "fair share" of the nation's tax collections to no more than it ought to be.

Your Advisor Must be Qualified

You may have been going to one of the nationwide tax preparation services to have your tax return done. These folks usually charge modestly for their work and promise that if you are called in for a tax audit, they can go with you to the IRS office to "explain" how your return was prepared.

Although these services employ many qualified and well-intentioned individuals who perform a valuable function in our country, you can run into three problems.

1) As the owner of a business, your tax situation will probably become more complicated every year. You sometimes find people in nationwide tax preparation firms who are not as trained as they should be in order to deal with your problems. They can miss tax breaks which you ought to have and may botch up other parts of your return.

2) These services concentrate on "preparation," not "planning." They may know how to put what on which form. But they may never have given a thought to how you could have saved taxes before you did what they're putting on the form. You need somebody who can tell you how to save taxes before you do something *and* can then fill out your tax return in the most advantageous manner.

3) Having your return "explained" during a tax audit is not anywhere near the same thing as taking your personal tiger to the audit (Chapter 24). You need someone who will argue your case, not explain where numbers came from. You probably won't get this kind of service from a firm which does nothing but prepare tax returns.

Instead of a nationwide preparation service, you could hire an independent preparer. These folks sometimes go by the title of "accountant" or "public accountant," but are not Certified Public Accountants. Such a person may do bookkeeping and tax work year 'round and is more likely to be able to provide the type of help you need than is the nationwide service.

If an accountant is rfot a Certified Public Accountant, you should ask around before letting him do work for you. Most areas of the U.S. require no tests or qualifications of people who want to go into business as bookkeepers or tax advisors. Consequently, the quality of the services you get may range from very bad to excellent.

Some of them will offer you the same three problems you could have with a nationwide tax service. You may receive what you pay for, but not really get what you need.

If you plan to pursue the maximum tax savings possible with your business, you may want to consider hiring a tax lawyer or a Certified Public Accountant (CPA). The lawyer has been through seven years of university schooling and passed his bar exam. The CPA has had four or five years of university education and has passed a rigorous two and one-half day CPA exam.

Be sure, however, that you hire someone who specializes in business taxes and does little else all year. Lawyers may handle everything from divorces to traffic cases to wills. CPA's may conduct financial audits or install computer systems. Tax law is too jealous a master to let a lawyer or CPA run around doing other things and, at the same time, keep completely up to date on tax changes.

You want a tax advisor—someone whom you can call at 3 p.m. Wednesday when you see a problem and who will give you a reasonably fast answer. You'll want the possibility of receiving tax-saving suggestions along with your answer. If your tax advisor has been handling divorces or audits for the past month, you may not get what you need when you need it.

CPA firms which have more than three partners often have enough tax business so that one partner can spend most of his time on taxes. Some law firms don't have any tax specialists; others have several.

Always ask how much of his time a lawyer or CPA devotes to taxes before you hire him. He may review the year's tax law changes in January and know exactly how to fill out your tax return when you see him in April. But what you want is someone who will keep the wrong things *off* your tax return when you call him in September. Next April is too late to change anything. Everything was made permanent at midnight, December 31.

How To Choose One

Not only should you choose an advisor who spends almost all his time on taxes, you'll want to be sure that other people are satisfied with his work. It is *your* money. And you are going to pay your advisor to help you keep as much of it as possible. So, you'd better know that he is doing his job for others.

Talk to your friends, acquaintances, bankers, brokers, insurance agents, and everyone else who knows tax advisors. Ask them who they use and whether or not they are satisfied with what they get.

Is he saving them money? Does he make tax-saving suggestions? Does he return their calls promptly (a real problem with some firms)? What does he charge? Does he get emotional under pressure? Is his office conveniently located? Is he too often out of town? Do clients' questions get delegated to underlings?

Make your top choice from among the tax people your sources recommend. Then go to visit him and ask exactly what he can do for you and when he can do it. Ask how much he charges and what your annual bill is likely to be. If this individual seems evasive on any of these points, you may want to look elsewhere. You'll be needing a straightforward, honest consultant when the chips are down.

Getting the Best for Less

Paying more does not always get you better advice in the tax field. The areas of expertise and billing rates of tax consultants can vary dramatically from one to the next. You should inquire about the person's experience and the area in which he presently does most of his work. You don't need a $200-an-hour expert on corporate reorganizations to tell you what types of business equipment will give you the most tax shelter. A low hourly rate will not guarantee you a bargain, but neither will a high rate necessarily get you the best advice available.

Unless you have an unusual problem, a CPA can probably give you what you need cheaper than can a lawyer. Lawyers often seem to charge more on an hourly basis. And many lawyers prefer not to prepare tax returns.

Even among CPA firms, you can pay widely different rates for the same work. You may want to stay away from extremely small firms. But neither should you go to the largest (unless you have a very complicated problem.). They have plush offices, country club memberships, and other high-overhead items to support.

Barring extremely technical questions about your business, you can probably find comparable advice for a lower price by seeking out a local CPA firm with four to twelve partners. This size firm undoubtedly has one or more veteran tax advisors who can give you excellent tax-saving advice. He can flawlessly fill out your tax forms in the way that will draw the least attention from the IRS. And he'll be a comfort and a competent defender in the event of an audit. You will pay more than you would for the services of a national tax return preparation service, but less than you would to a large CPA firm or law firm. You'll probably get your money's worth.

Talk Now, Act Later

Now that you've found an advisor, how can you best use him?

Although you are forced to buy certain items for your business during the year—inventory, insurance, salaries—it is easy to postpone seeing your tax advisor about tax planning. You may not feel as though you have the time.

The idea of a tax advisor also conjures up unpleasant recollections of tax seasons and feelings of helplessness which come from writing big checks to the IRS. In fact, many people wonder what benefit they actually receive from their tax consultants.

But the time to talk to your tax expert about how to postpone income or to increase deductions is *before* the end of the year. After December 31, it is too late. You are locked in to what's already happened.

Surely, there is time for at least one quick conference during your tax advisor's off season—usually the late summer and fall—to discuss your current year's tax situation. Such a conversation will allow you to take a variety of tax-saving actions before the end of the year.

Likewise, a 15-minute chat by phone before you commit yourself to a deal can yield low-cost peace of mind and can even encourage the service-oriented advisor to call later with some year-end tax tips.

These contacts with your tax consultant—when he has the time to devote his full attention to your problems and possibilities—can cost much less than your potential tax savings.

If your business is large enough to justify a full-time accountant or controller, try to hire one who will think in terms of taxes every day. Be sure to include him in the planning of all fair-sized transactions. Such an employee may be able to save you more in taxes each year than you pay him in salary.

When you think of taxes as an expense of your business (perhaps your largest expense) regular contact with the one person who can reduce it makes sense. If you see him only during tax season, you are likely to get exactly what you pay for—the hurried preparation of a tax return for a year whose income and deductions were set in concrete on December 31.

No Time for You?

Does your tax advisor fail to return your calls as soon as he should? This is a frequently-heard complaint about professional people.

When you finally reach him, does he say, "I'll have to look into that and get back to you," but is slow about doing so?

Perhaps you bring up the various tax-saving techniques explained in this book, but (without exploring further) he says in an off-hand manner that he doesn't think you are eligible for any of them.

Your tax situation may be ripe for additional tax breaks that nobody is telling you about.

Your tax advisor is *your* employee. If he does not have time to do a good job for you, find another. There are plenty of good CPA's and lawyers out there who are willing to break their backs to get your business.

A carpenter earns his living with saws and hammers—tools of his trade. The tools you use to increase your wealth and move toward financial well-being are capital, business know-how, and expert advisors. If one of your tools is not always available or cooperative when you need it, how are you going to do the best you can with what you've got?

Important Points

It is important to work *with* your tax advisor all year. If you see him only when it is time to prepare your tax return, you may be missing out on some excellent tax-saving opportunities. No amount of subsequent thought or anxiety can change what is locked in when people begin singing "Auld Lang Syne."

A good tax advisor can save you a lot more in taxes than his fees cost you. So, be sure to do your homework before you hire one. Find his satisfied—and dissatisfied—customers and pump them for information. Determine what the annual costs of his services will be and ascertain exactly what he can and cannot do for you.

And do not automatically hire the most expensive consultant available. Unless you have some unusual problems, you probably don't need him.

You can find many highly qualified tax advisors who will cost you less than the "best," but who can give you valuable advice when you need it. They spend a large part of each day involved in tax planning and preparation and keep up with the torrent of changes in tax rules. They will answer your questions when you need them answered and will tell you realistically what you can do to lower your tax bill. They'll help you to keep income off your tax return and generate more deductions to put on it.

If your advisor becomes too busy to give you the type of service you need, find another. A consultant who does not help you save taxes as he should may end up being a lot more expensive than one who'll do his job properly.

In the final analysis, no one has as much at stake in your business as you do. It is up to you to be aware of the tax-saving methods explained in this book and to see that your business takes advantage of them. Thinking about saving taxes as you go through each day will become a habit. And you *will* save taxes.

The whole area of taxes is one expense of your business that you can successfully reduce. And now you know exactly how to do it.

Appendices

Appendix   A

Mileage Log

Date	Locations Visited	Purpose of Visit	Beginning Mileage	Ending Mileage	Total Distance

Appendix   B

Expense Diary		Specific Location of Expenditure	Names and Titles of People Visited	Purpose of Expenditure	Type of Expenditure (Entertainment, Cab Fare, Etc.)
Date	Amount				

Appendix C

Business Gifts

Date	Recipient's Name and Title	Business Relationship	Reason Gift	Cost of Gift	Description of Gift

Appendix   D

Selected IRS Forms

Schedule A, Itemized Deductions

Schedule B, Interest Income (if more than $400 or if from All-Savers
            Certificates)
            Dividends and Other Distributions on Stock (if more
            than $400)
            Foreign Accounts or Foreign Trusts Questions

Schedule C, Income from a Personally Owned Business

Schedule D, Income from the Sale or Exchange of Capital Assets

Schedule E, Income from Rents, Royalties, Partnerships, Estates,
            Trusts, Etc.

Schedule F, Income from Farming

Schedule G, Income Averaging

Schedule SE, Reporting Net Earnings from Self-Employment

Form 1040-ES, Estimated Tax Payments

Form 1040-X, Amended Individual Income Tax Return

Form 1065, Partnership Tax Return

Form 1120, Corporation Tax Return

Form 2106, Employee Business Expenses

Form 2119, Sale or Exchange of Principal Residence

Form 2210, Underpayment of Estimated Tax by Individuals

Form 2858, Application for Automatic Extension of Time to File
            U.S. Partnership Return

Form 3468, Computation of Investment Credit

Form 3903, Moving Expense Adjustment

Form 4136, Computation of Credit for Federal Tax on Gasoline,
            Special Fuels, and Lubricating Oil

Form 4562, Depreciation

Form 4684, Casualties and Thefts

Form 4797, Supplemental Schedule of Gains and Losses

Form 4835, Farm Rental Income and Expenses

Form 4868, Application for Automatic Extension of Time to File U.S. Individual Income Tax Return

Form 6251, Alternative Minimum Tax Computation

Form 7004, Application for Automatic Extension of Time to File U.S. Corporate Tax Return

Appendix   E

Selected IRS Publications

Appendix   F

Telephone Numbers of IRS Offices

Alabama

Birmingham 252-1155
Huntsville 539-2751
Montgomery 264-8441
Other Alabama Areas 1-800-292-6300

Alaska

Anchorage 276-1040
Other Alaska Areas .... call operator and ask for Zenith 3700

Arizona

Phoenix 257-1233
Tucson 882-4181
Other Arizona Areas 1-800-352-6911

Arkansas

Little Rock 376-4401
Other Arkansas Areas 1-800-482-9350

California

If you live in California, the IRS asks that you
look under "U.S. Government, Internal Revenue
Service, Federal Tax Assistance" in the white
pages of your local telephone book.

Colorado

Denver 825-7041
Other Colorado Areas 1-800-332-2060

Connecticut

All Areas 1-800-343-9000

Delaware

Wilmington 573-6400
Other Delaware Areas 1-800-292-9575

District of Columbia

All Areas 488-3100

Florida

Fort Lauderdale 522-0704
Jacksonville 354-1760
Miami 358-5072
Orlando 422-2550
St. Petersburg 823-7459
Tampa 223-9741
West Palm Beach 655-7250
Other Florida Areas 1-800-342-8300

Georgia

Atlanta 522-0050
Augusta 724-9946
Columbus 327-7491
Macon 746-4993
Savannah 355-1045
Other Georgia Areas 1-800-222-1040

Hawaii

Hawaii 935-4895
Oahu 546-8660
Kauai 245-2731
Lanai .... call operator and ask for .... Enterprise 8036
Maui 244-7654
Molokai .... call operator and ask for .... Enterprise 8034

Idaho

Boise 336-1040
Other Idaho Areas 1-800-632-5990

Illinois

Chicago 435-1040
Other Illinois Areas 1-800-972-5400

Indiana

Evansville 424-6481
Fort Wayne 426-8300
Gary 938-0560
Hammond 938-0560
Indianapolis 269-5477
South Bend 232-3981
Other Indiana Areas 1-800-382-9740

Iowa

Des Moines 284-4850
Other Iowa Areas 1-800-362-2600

Kansas

Wichita 263-2161
Other Kansas Areas 1-800-362-2190

Kentucky

Lexington 255-2333
Louisville 584-1361
Northern Kentucky (Covington Dialing Area) 628-0055
Other Kentucky Areas 1-800-428-9100

Louisiana

New Orleans 581-2440
Other Louisiana Areas 1-800-362-6900

Maine

Augusta 622-7101
Other Maine Areas 1-800-452-8750

Maryland

Baltimore 962-2590
Prince Georges County 488-3100
Montgomery County 488-3100
Other Maryland Areas 1-800-492-0460

Massachusetts

Boston 523-1040
Other Massachusetts Areas 1-800-392-6288

Michigan

Ann Arbor 769-9850
Detroit 237-0800
Flint 767-8830
Grand Rapids 774-8300
Mount Clemens 469-4200
Pontiac 858-2530
Other Michigan Areas (Area Code 313) 1-800-462-0830
Other Michigan Areas (Area Code 517, 616, 906) 1-800-482-0670

Minnesota

Minneapolis 291-1422
St. Paul 291-1422
Other Minnesota Areas 1-800-652-9062

Mississippi

Biloxi 868-2122
Gulfport 868-2122
Jackson 948-4500
Other Mississippi Areas 1-800-241-3868

Missouri

St. Louis 342-1040
Other Missouri Areas 1-800-392-4200

Montana

Helena 443-2320
Other Montana Areas 1-800-332-2275

Nebraska

Omaha 422-1500
Other Nebraska Areas 1-800-642-9960

Nevada

Las Vegas 385-6291
Reno 784-5521
Other Nevada Areas 1-800-492-6552

New Hampshire

Portsmouth 436-8810
Other New Hampshire Areas 1-800-582-7200

New Jersey

Camden 966-7333
Hackensack.. 646-1919
Jersey City 622-0600
Newark 622-0600
Paterson 279-9400
Trenton 394-7113
Other New Jersey Areas 1-800-242-6750

New Mexico

Albuquerque 243-8641
Other New Mexico Areas 1-800-527-3880

New York

Albany District (Eastern Upstate New York) 1-800-343-9000
Brooklyn 596-3770
Nassau 294-3600
Queens 596-3770
Suffolk 724-5000
Buffalo 855-3955
Rochester 263-6770
Syracuse 425-8111
Other Central and Western New York Areas 1-800-462-1560
Bronx.. 732-0100
Manhattan 732-0100

Rockland County 352-8900
Staten Island 732-0100
Westchester County 997-1510

North Carolina

Charlotte 372-7750
Greensboro 274-3711
Raleigh 828-6278
Other North Carolina Areas 1-800-822-8800

North Dakota

Fargo 293-0650
Other North Dakota Areas 1-800-342-4710

Ohio

Akron 253-1141
Canton 455-6781
Cincinnati 621-6281
Cleveland 522-3000
Columbus 228-0520
Dayton 228-0557
Toledo 255-3730
Youngstown 746-1811
Other Northern Ohio Areas 1-800-362-9050
Other Southern Ohio Areas 1-800-582-1700

Oklahoma

Oklahoma City 272-9531
Tulsa 583-5121
Other Oklahoma Areas 1-800-962-3456

Oregon

Eugene 485-8285

Medford 779-3375
Portland 221-3960
Salem 581-8720
Other Oregon Areas 1-800-452-1980

Pennsylvania

Allentown 437-6966
Bethlehem 437-6966
Erie 453-5671
Harrisburg 783-8700
Philadelphia 574-9900
Pittsburgh 281-0112
Other Pennsylvania Areas (Area Code 215, 717) 1-800-462-4000
Other Pennsylvania Areas (Area Code 412, 814) 1-800-242-0250

Rhode Island

Providence 274-1040
Other Rhode Island Areas 1-800-662-5055

South Carolina

Charleston 722-1601
Columbia 799-1040
Greenville 242-5434
Other South Carolina Areas 1-800-241-3868

South Dakota

Aberdeen 225-9112
Other South Dakota Areas 1-800-592-1870

Tennessee

Chattanooga 756-3010
Knoxville 637-0190
Memphis 522-1250

Nashville 259-4601
Other Tennessee Areas 1-800-342-8420

Texas

Austin 472-1974
Corpus Christi 888-9431
Dallas 742-2440
El Paso 532-6116
Ft. Worth 335-1370
Houston 965-0440
San Antonio 229-1700
Other Texas Areas 1-800-492-4830

Utah

Salt Lake City 524-4060
Other Utah Areas 1-800-662-5370

Vermont

Burlington 658-1870
Other Vermont Areas 1-800-642-3110

Virginia

Baileys Crossroads (Northern Virginia) 557-9230
Chesapeake 461-3770
Norfolk 461-3770
Portsmouth 461-3770
Richmond 649-2361
Virginia Beach 461-3770
Other Virginia Areas 1-800-552-9500

Washington

Everett 259-0861
Seattle 442-1040

Spokane 456-8350
Tacoma 383-2021
Other Washington Areas 1-800-732-1040

West Virginia

Charleston 345-2210
Huntington 523-0213
Parkersburg 485-1601
Wheeling 233-4210
Other West Virginia Areas 1-800-543-7200

Wisconsin

Milwaukee 271-3780
Other Wisconsin Areas 1-800-452-9100

Wyoming

All Areas 1-800-525-6060

Index

We'd Like to Hear from You!

Dear Reader,

As part of our continuing efforts to publish books of the highest quality, Enterprise Publishing, Inc. invites you to share your thinking about this book. We plan to use the information you provide to help us to serve our readers better as we revise and update this book in future editions.

Please take a minute or two to answer the following:

Why did you buy this book?

What did you like most about it?

What did you like least?

Have you personally benefited from reading this? If so, in what way?

Will you recommend this book to a friend or colleague? Why or why not?

Other comments you'd like to make about this book?

What other books have you purchased in the past 3 months?

_____   _____

_____   _____

Where did you buy this book?

         ☐ Bookstore   ☐ Mail Order   ☐ Other _____

City/State in which you reside: _____ Your age: _____

Your sex: _____   Your occupation: _____

Your name & address (optional): _____

May we use your name in future advertising and publicity?   ☐ Yes   ☐ No

Thank you for sharing your comments.

Please clip this page and mail to:

ENTERPRISE PUBLISHING, INC.
DEPARTMENT B
725 MARKET STREET
WILMINGTON, DELAWARE 19801